MW01620543

A coyote peered beguilingly from the shadow of her spring hat—a flamboyant jumble of blooming cacti and wildflowers. Prickly pear cactus pads, Christmas cholla, Mojave asters, hesperaloe and desert spoon leaves, blackfoot daisies, Southwest coral bean, prickly poppy, acacia, spiny daisies, and dangling velvet mesquite pods were fancied up with a snakeskin bow. An Apache jumping spider planned his next move. Milkweed stems with sage leaves formed a necklace, while a desert checkered skipper poised on a strand of creosote seeds.

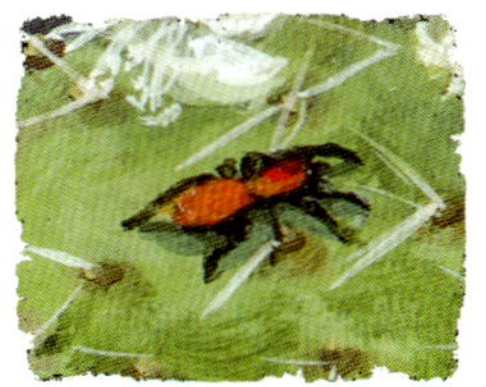

The Wild Hat

A Fable of Fashion Intrigue in the Desert

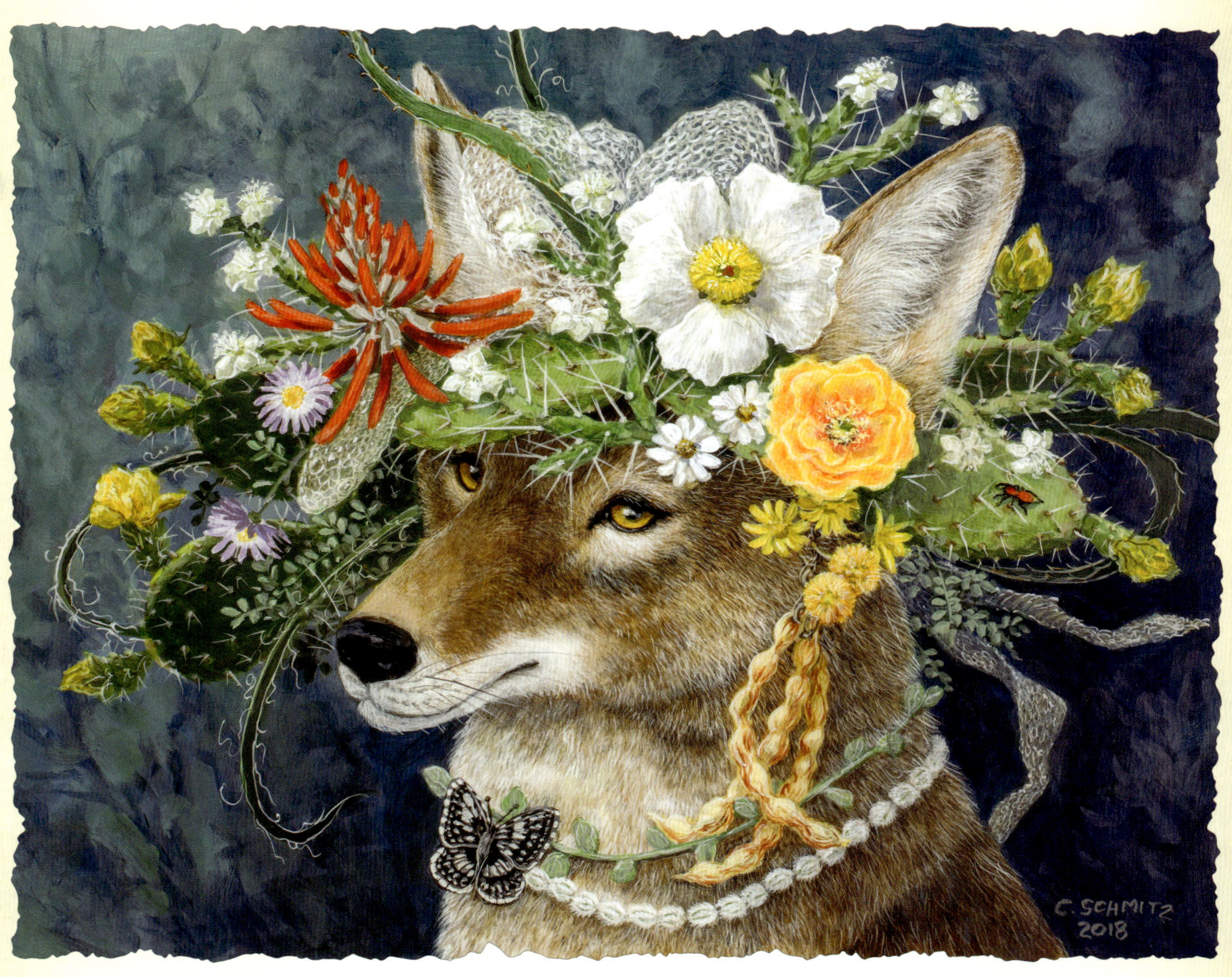

Story and Paintings by Carolyn Schmitz

Published by Desert Dada® Press

Book design by Tony Schmitz

ISBN 978-0-578-49812-6

Library of Congress Control Number:2019906601

www.desertdada.com desertdada@gmail.com

For My Parents

Their hard work and tremendous sacrifice made my idyllic childhood in the forest and the desert possible. That life, along with Leo's zany humor and Pauline's playful spirit and love of art inspired me to become an artist. I am grateful to them every day.

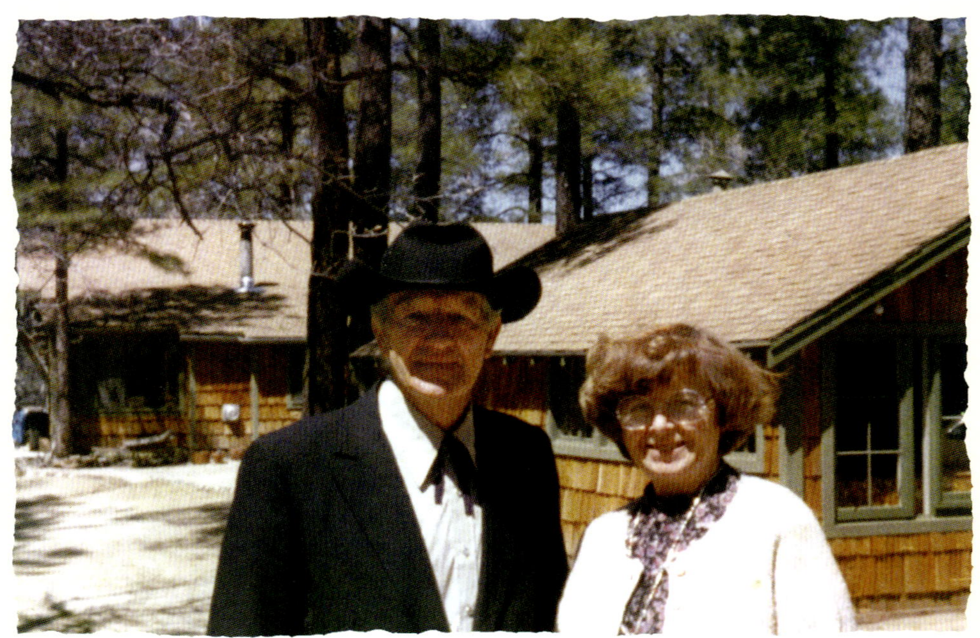

Leo and Pauline Schmitz, Prescott, Arizona

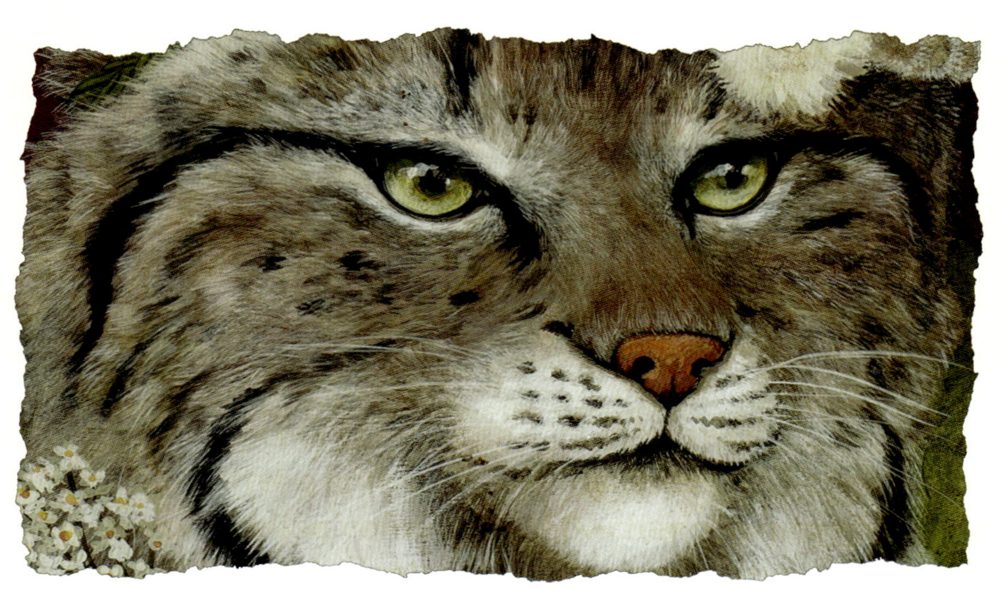

Introduction / Meditation

It is my great joy to have lived most of my life in virgin landscapes—to walk out the door into a ponderosa pine forest, a flowering meadow, or a rocky arroyo lined with cacti. Roaming about in the hills, I discovered small things in the shadow of my hat as breathtaking as any panorama. I met new plants and greeted familiar ones, made eye contact with lizards and furry folk, wondering what they had been up to in the course of their lives.

In painting the resident wildlife embellished with the flora of their native habitats, I suggest that the boundary between them and us is a fuzzy one. (So to speak.) In order to survive, all of us—plants too!—endure, adapt, invent, cooperate, compete, and deceive. Or even dress up and show off! We are all Beings, expressing life in uncountable unique ways.

Our animal relatives modelling hats is an amusing way to see ourselves in them and them in us, while celebrating the beauty and diversity of our earth's marvelous botanical and zoological garden.

Sister Mary Elizabeth told me in 7th grade that I would write a book someday. This must be it.

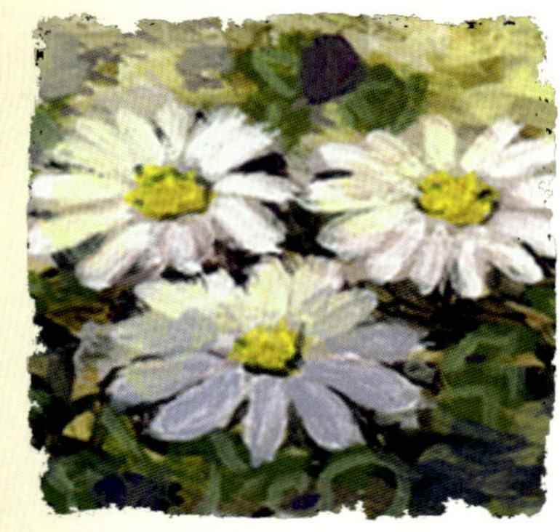

Everyone suspected the ravens. That impossible gathering of both predator and prey under a desert moon had a hint of chicanery, not chance. Though the dust had long since settled, there was still "talk."

An elderly Gila monster couple, dressed comfortably in jumpsuits beaded with obsidian and rose quartz, dragged their agave lounges to a sunny spot among cholla, bahia, and daisy-like desert stars. Gazing dreamily at a dust devil spinning across the flats, they recalled the event that had happened merely a moon ago.

"What a heady time," he laughed.

"It was crazy!" she gasped. "Madness caused by those bratty birds!"

"QUONK!" A raven startled them from an ironwood tree. "Lighten up, you two beanbags. It was fun!"

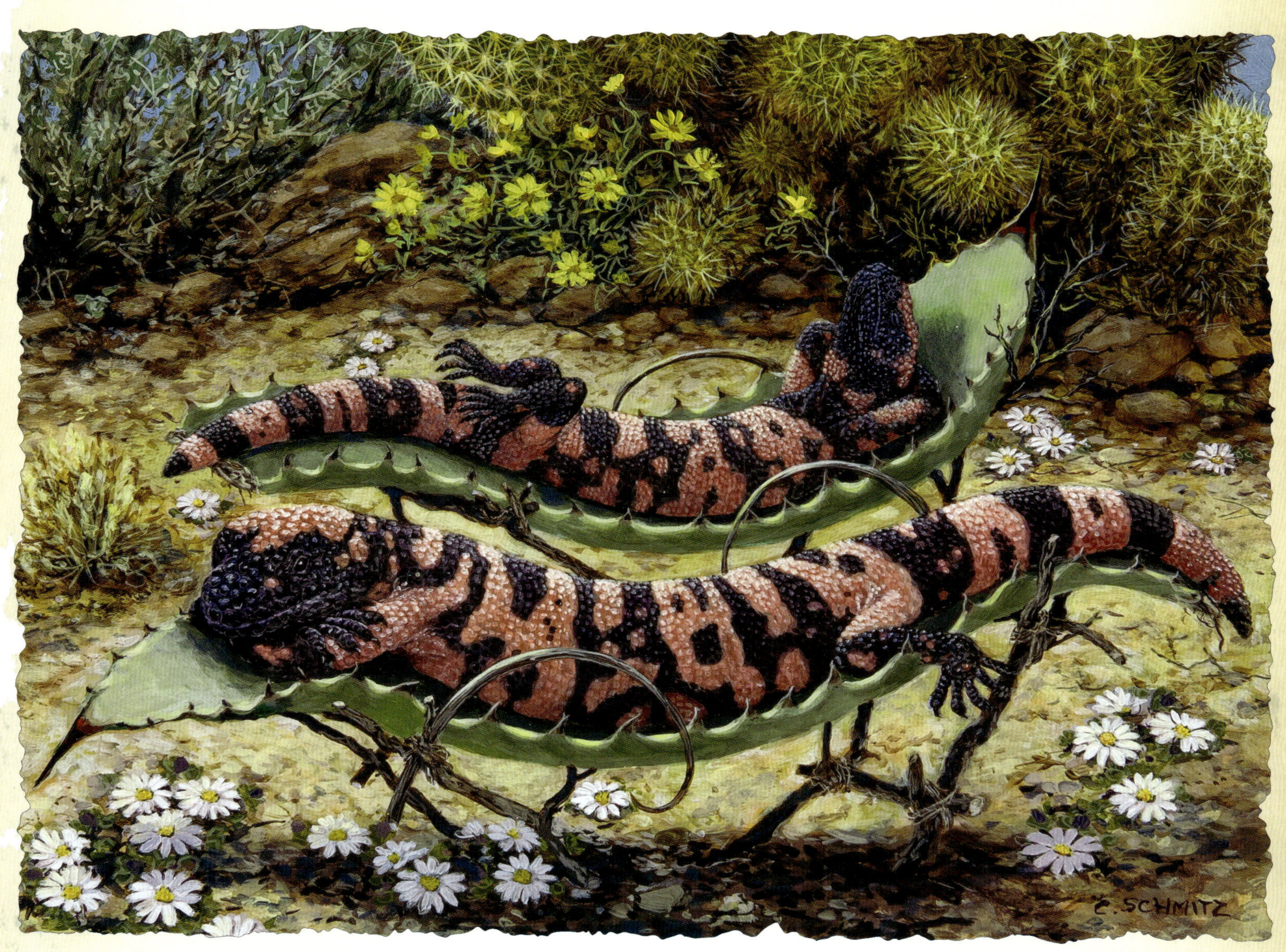
E. SCHMITZ

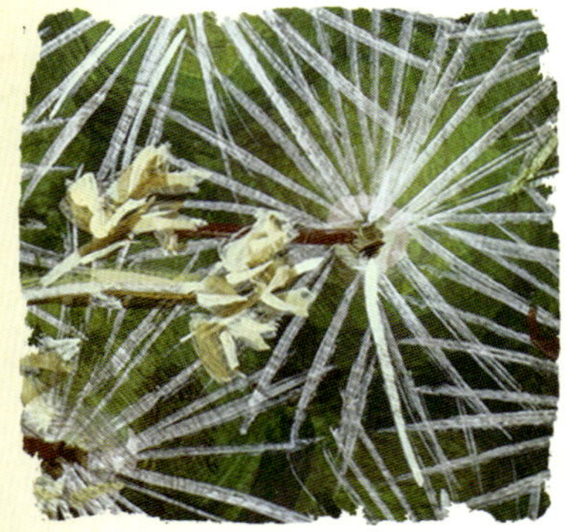

Perhaps it was miraculous. Miracles were as common as stickers in the Sonoran Desert—most notably in spring. That's when this land of tough, spiny, pointy, gray-green plants did something shockingly out of character—it exhaled radiant colors.

Like a quiet symphony, puffs, frills, fans, twists, tassels, and spirals thrummed in the sunlight. As the night-blooms opened, dots of pale yellow and white chimed in the dark.

Even the sand sang with color!

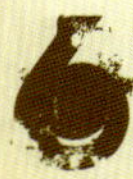

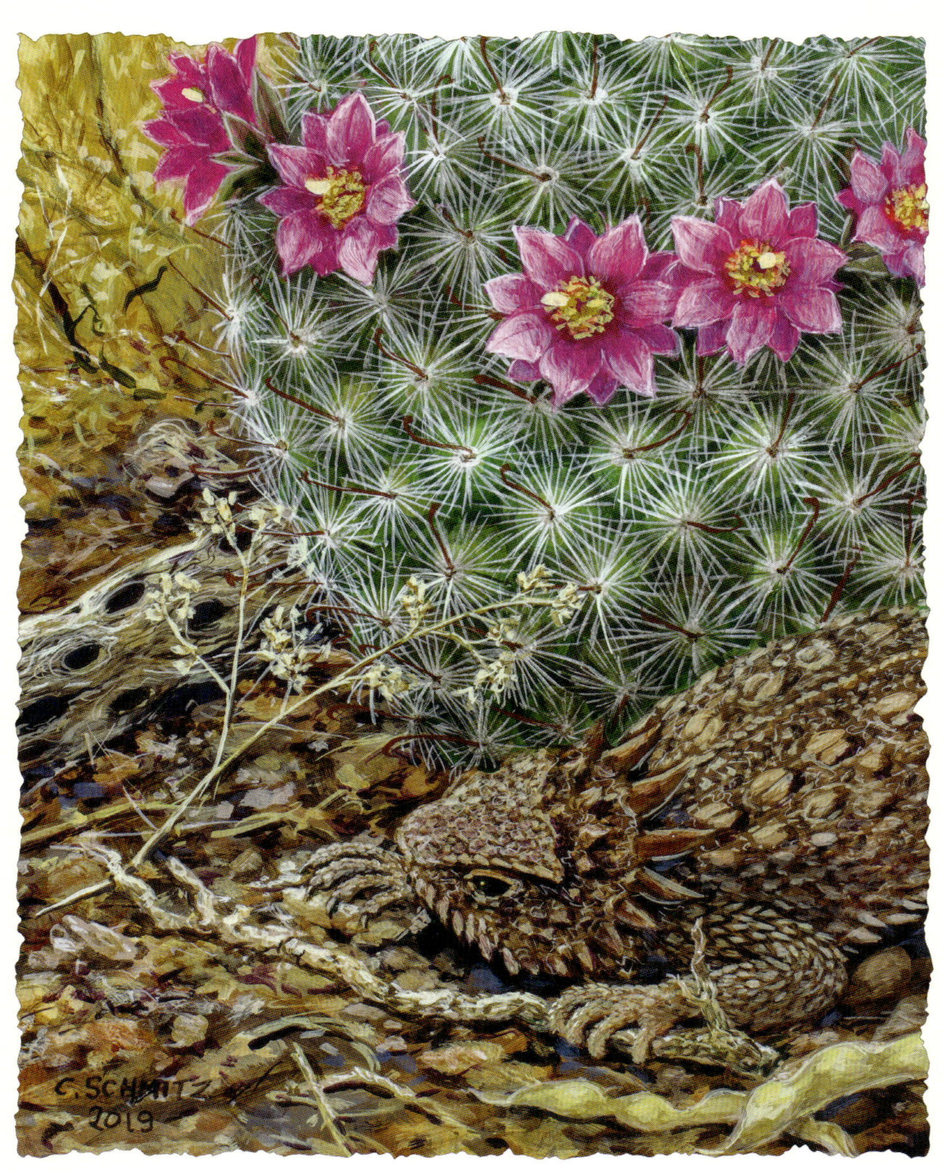
G. SCHMITZ
2019

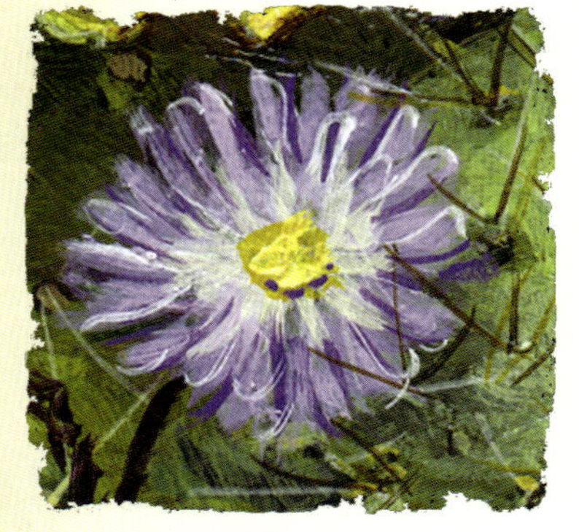

Or was it the ravens' doing? On one such spring day, a baby javelina rested in the shade of a blooming cactus amid a tangle of wildflowers—blackfoot daisies, desert trumpets, chinchweed, Mojave aster, angel trumpets, and globemallow. He was spied by a raven making his rounds of social calls.

"How odd," thought the bird. "He's wearing a cactus pad for a hat."

It wasn't long before the gossipy bird had broadcast what he'd just seen to everyone in the territory.

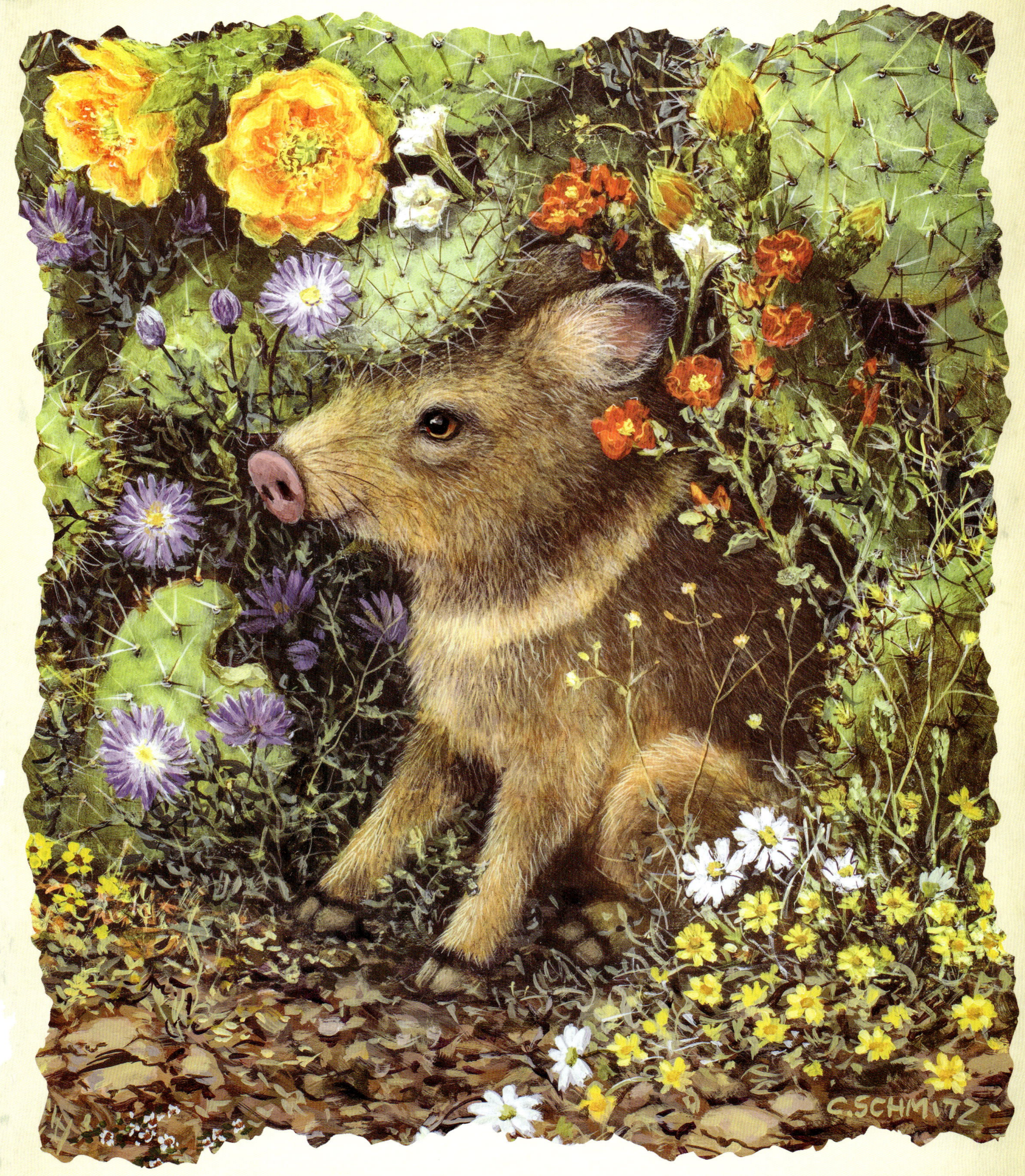

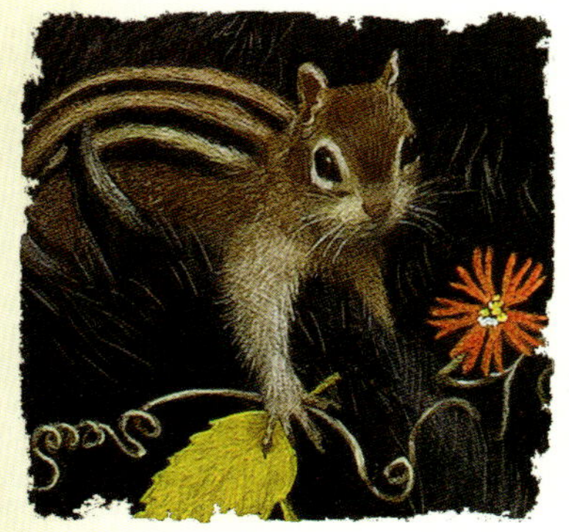

As the hat sighting was tossed about among the animals they became increasingly curious.

"Maybe the javelinas just wanted to spiff up their scruffy kids," a deer speculated.

"I'd love to wear a hat," said a coyote.

"I'd never be caught dead in a hat," grumbled a badger.

"Why wear stuff I could eat?" objected a ground squirrel.

More animals joined the spirited discussion. "How can we make hats?" asked those with hooves and paws.

"You can't," barked a raccoon.

"Relax," said a roadrunner. "A hat is just an artsy upside-down nest."

"KRAAA!" A raven got everyone's attention. "Let's have a costume ball! A competition!"

Seeing an opportunity to one-up each other, the animals cheered. They agreed upon a broad clearing ringed by fissured granite as the ideal place, with a bright April moon to enhance the evening activities.

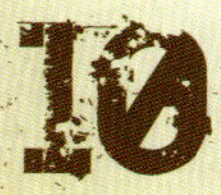

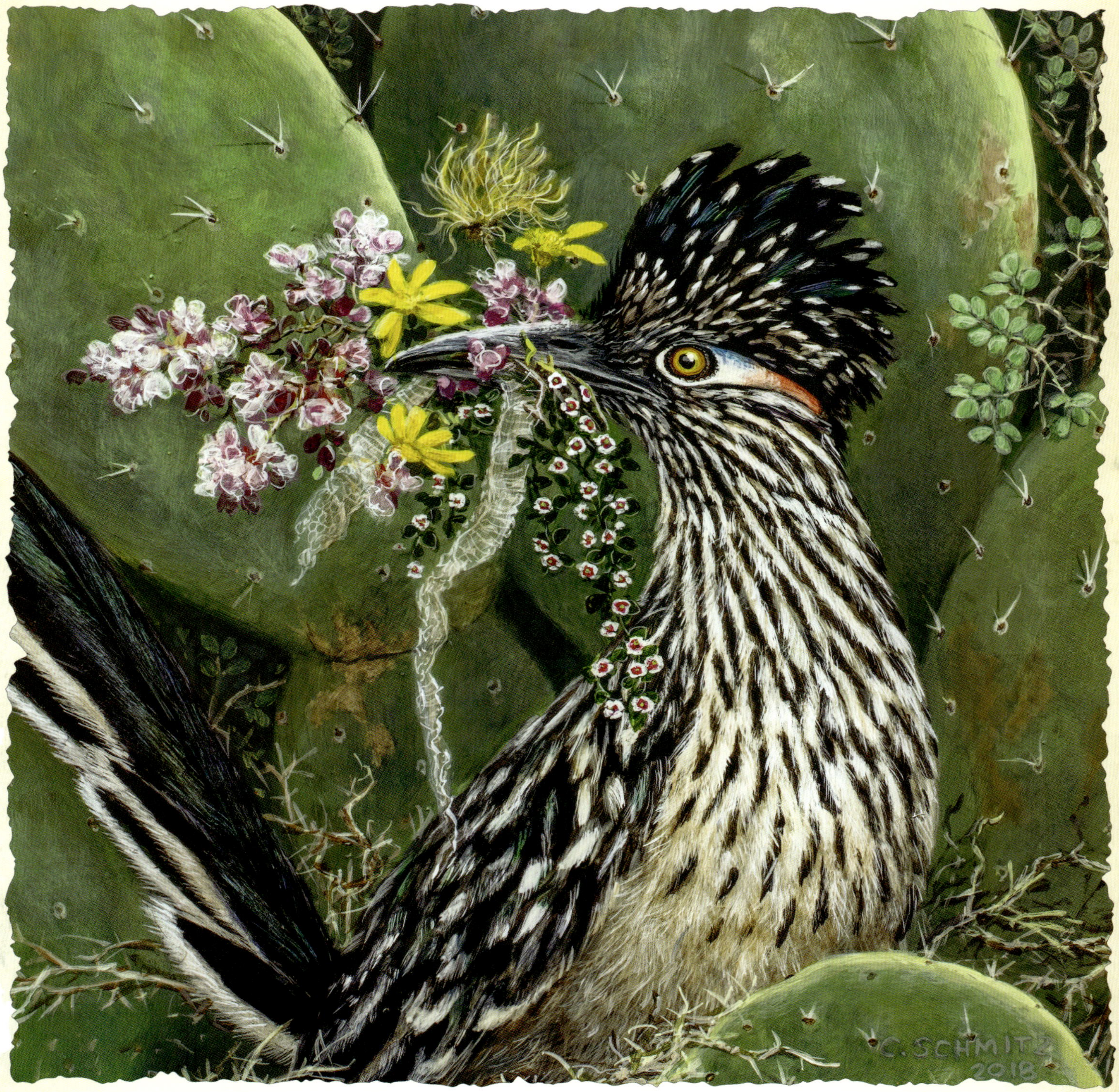

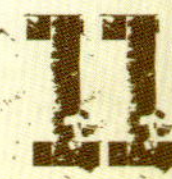
11

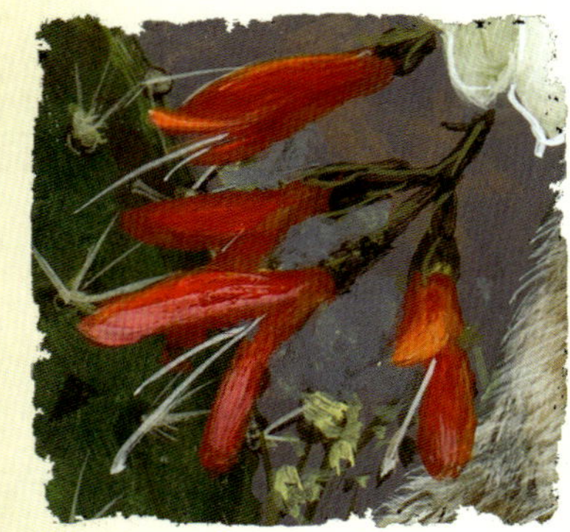

The ravens took off like black jets, inviting everyone via their extensive noisy network. Honks, chortles, screams, squonks, and raucous caws were heard by every desert dweller.

"From bite-size to bigger guys!" the birds chanted.

One raven placed a saguaro blossom and sprigs of chuparosa between the ears of a jackrabbit. Inspired and excited, the animals began fashioning their frippery from the abundance of materials right under their noses.

The rodents refrained from noshing on the supplies.

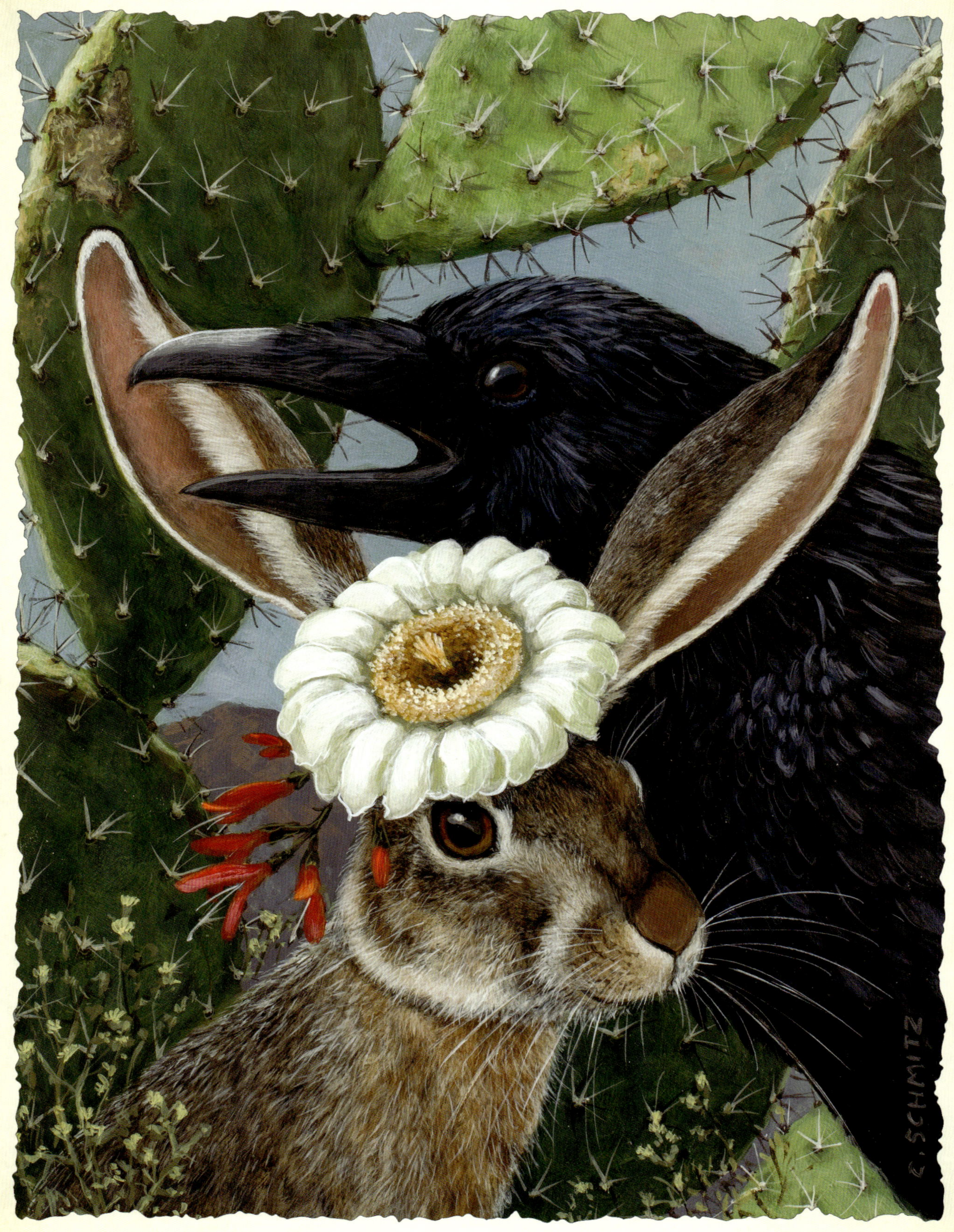
C. SCHMITZ

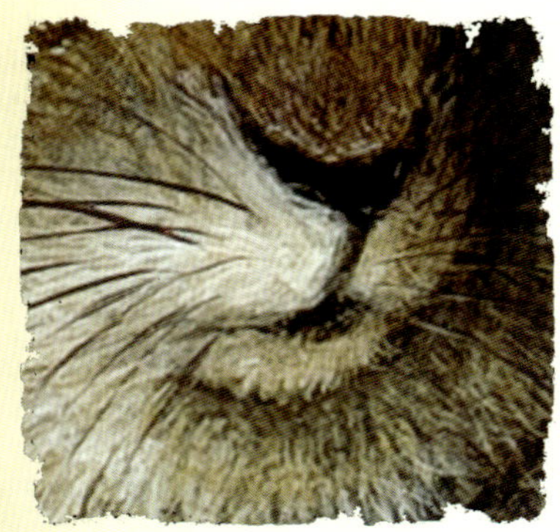

Advertising a sizable rummage sale, a Harris' antelope squirrel twirled a parasol—saguaro crust on a mesquite twig brightened up with acacia, desert fern, and fairy duster blossoms, then trimmed with scallops of scorpion tails.

"I knew those rodents were hoarders," a thrasher confided to her mate as they browsed among husks, hulls, pods, insect parts and assorted unmentionables.

The snakes, who could not make or wear hats, participated by selling their discarded skins. "Sheer keratin!" they called out to the shoppers. "Imagine the possibilities!"

Also offered for barter, in a secluded location, were rattlesnake rattles. Pricey and fragile, they were of dubious provenance.

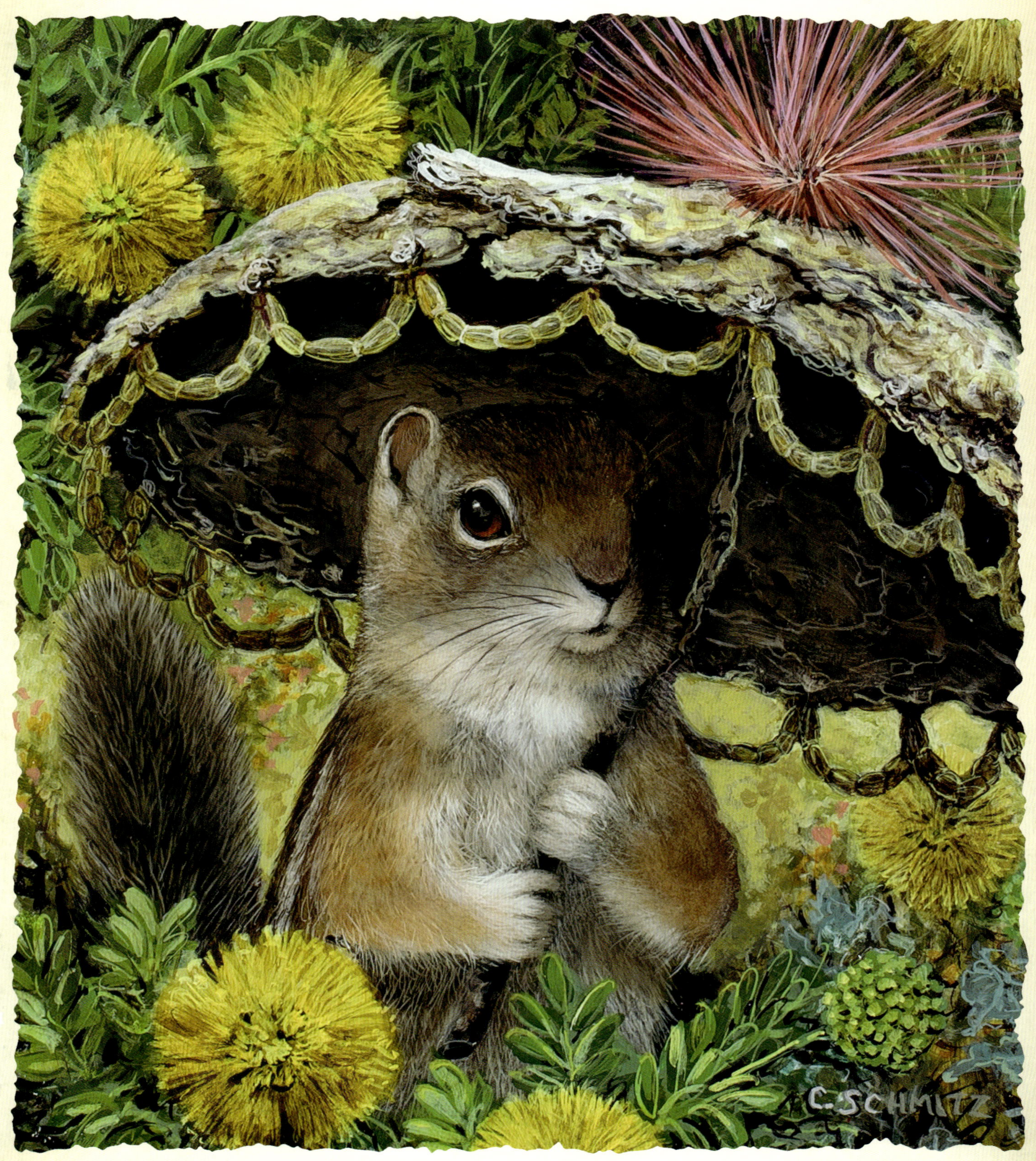
C.SCHMITZ

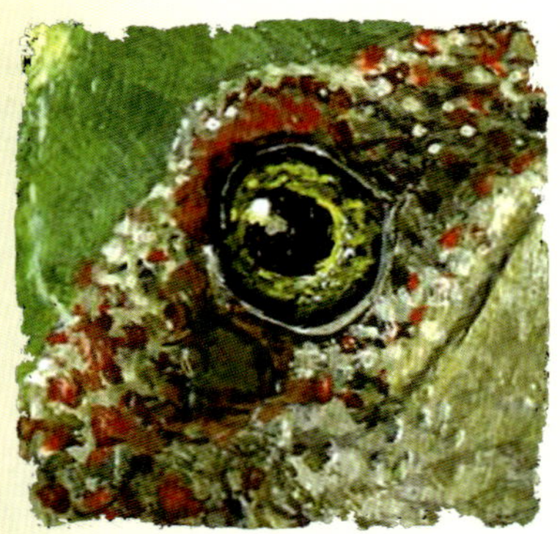

A red-spotted toad and a Harris' antelope squirrel took advantage of a spring downpour to arrive by boat. With a banner of mesquite blossoms flying at the helm of their little skiff, they bounced along the current, not knowing how far it would take them before it fizzled out in the sand.

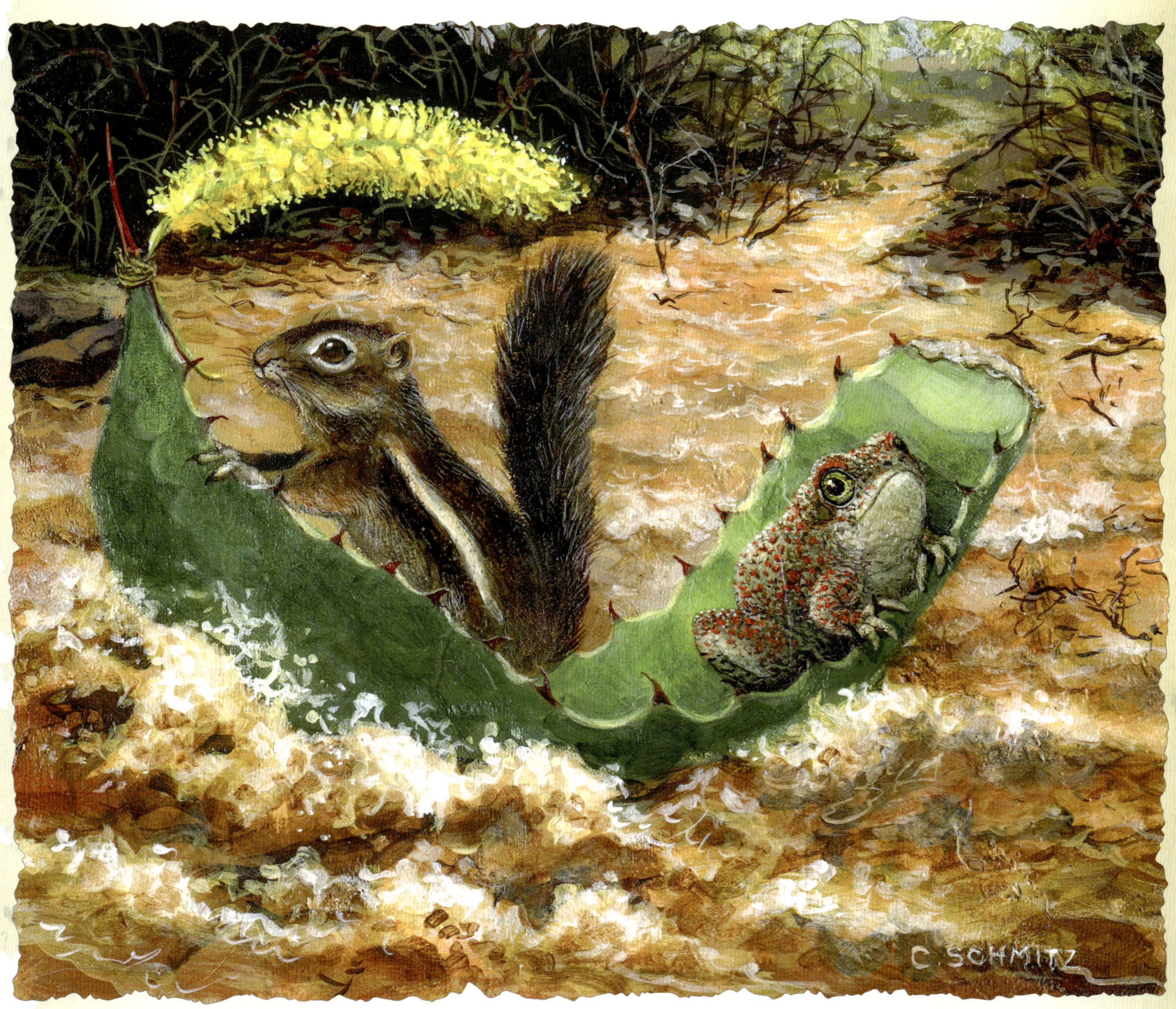
C. SCHMITZ

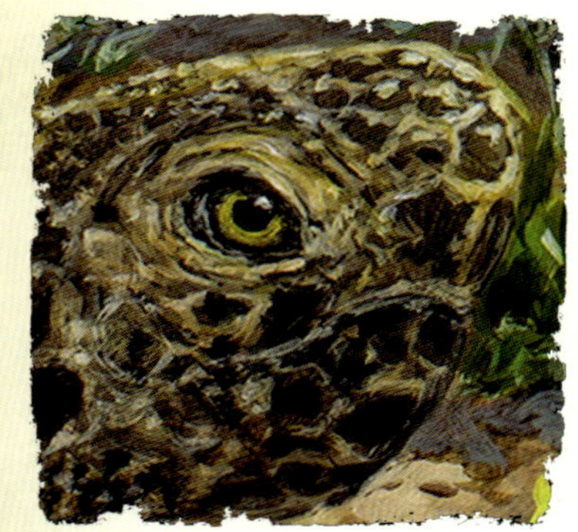

As the cliffs rose from deep indigo into gold on that April morning, creatures zigzagged into the clearing from all directions. An upstanding—so to speak—Gila monster couple, as judge and master of ceremonies, plopped onto their lounges. She wore an eye-popping pink and charcoal embroidered pantsuit and he a spangled hematite and coral unitard. Their sidekick Ed, a desert tortoise, was "on hand" for chuckles and dry commentary.

Gila Woodpeckers high in the saguaros made percussive sounds to herald the start of the festivities, while Cactus Wrens provided background music with their raspy voices.

"We were expecting *Canyon* Wrens," whispered the tortoise to the emcee.

He shrugged. "There must have been a mix-up."

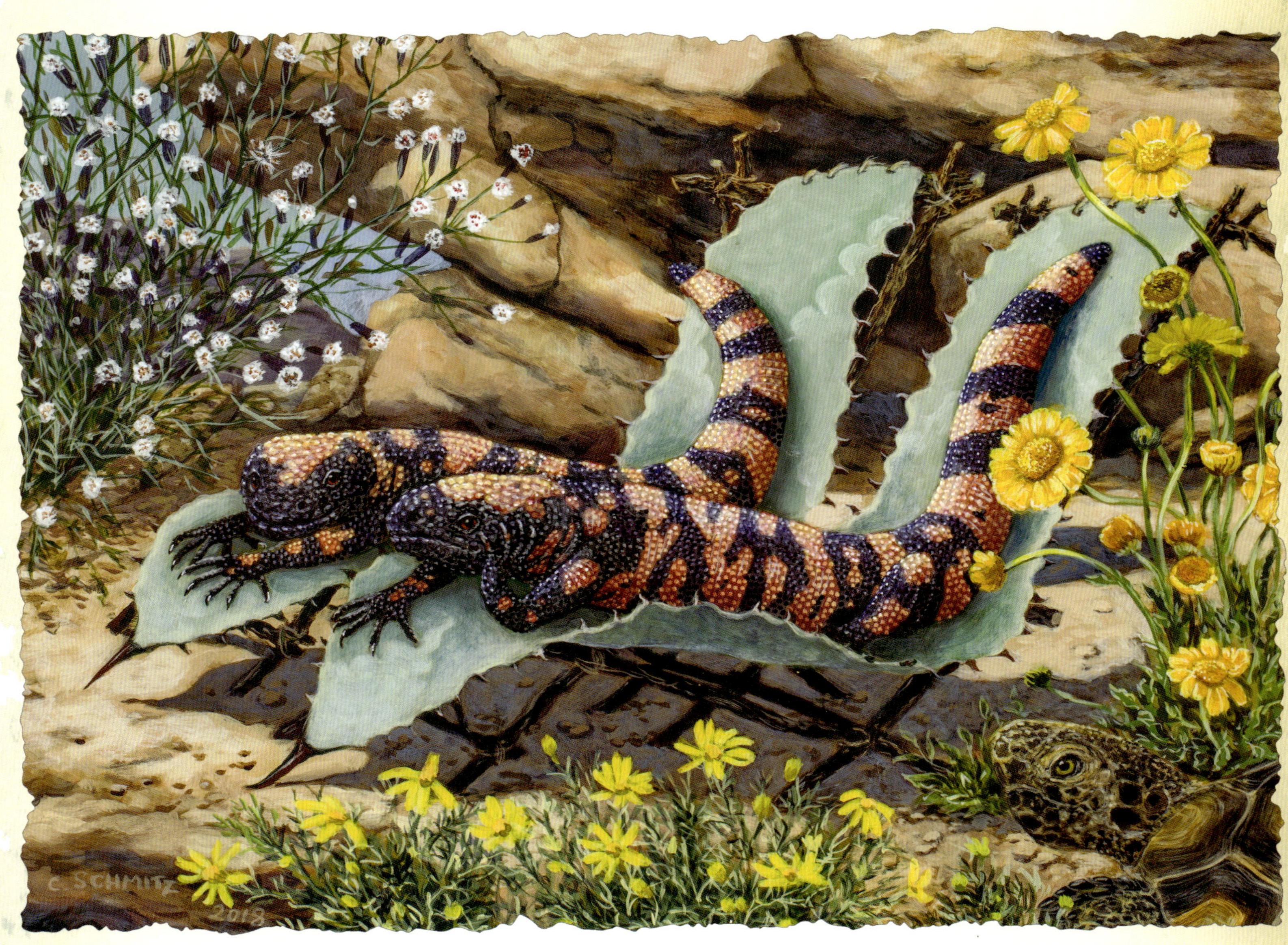
C. SCHMITZ
2018

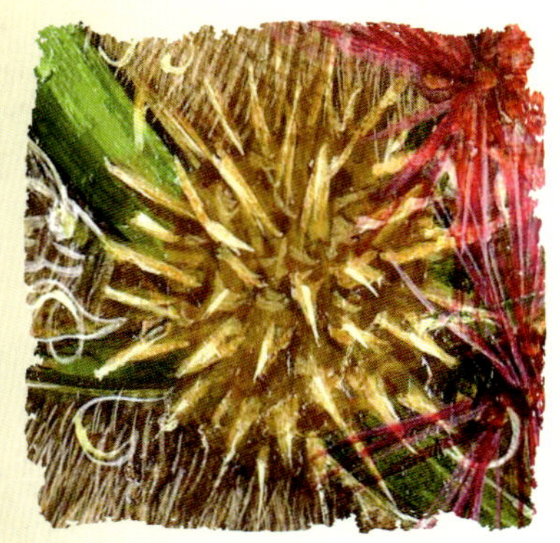

First to hop in from the desert scrub was a jackrabbit, festooned with rays of agave leaves to complement his ears, a cluster of prickly pear cactus, and a dramatic devil's claw spiral. A swath of snakeskin was accented with creosote seeds, fairy duster blooms, and yucca leaves. Fastened to his ears were the dried pods of datura and fairy duster.

"Surely I will chew up the competition!" he thought.

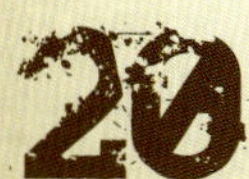

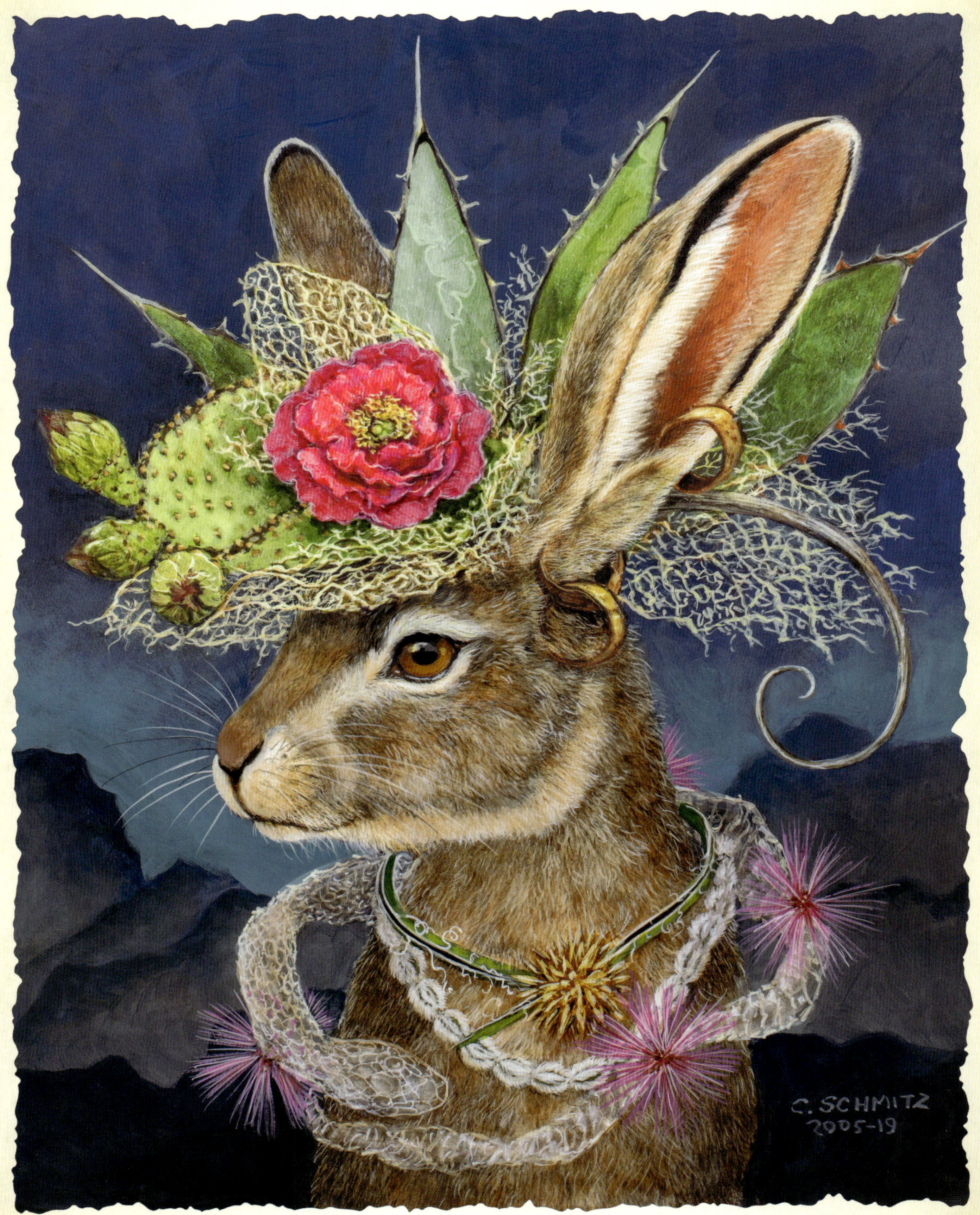
C. SCHMITZ
2005-19

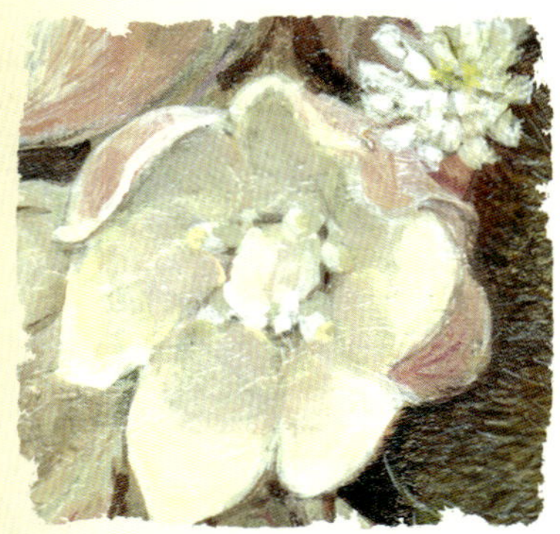

Loping in from Death Valley, a coyote posed elegantly in a cascade of Mojave yucca leaves and blossoms, with accents of devil's claws, buckwheat, and gravel ghost flowers. A sprinkle of Mojave desert stars across her neck and shoulders convinced her that simplicity and grace would win her the award for the loveliest hat.

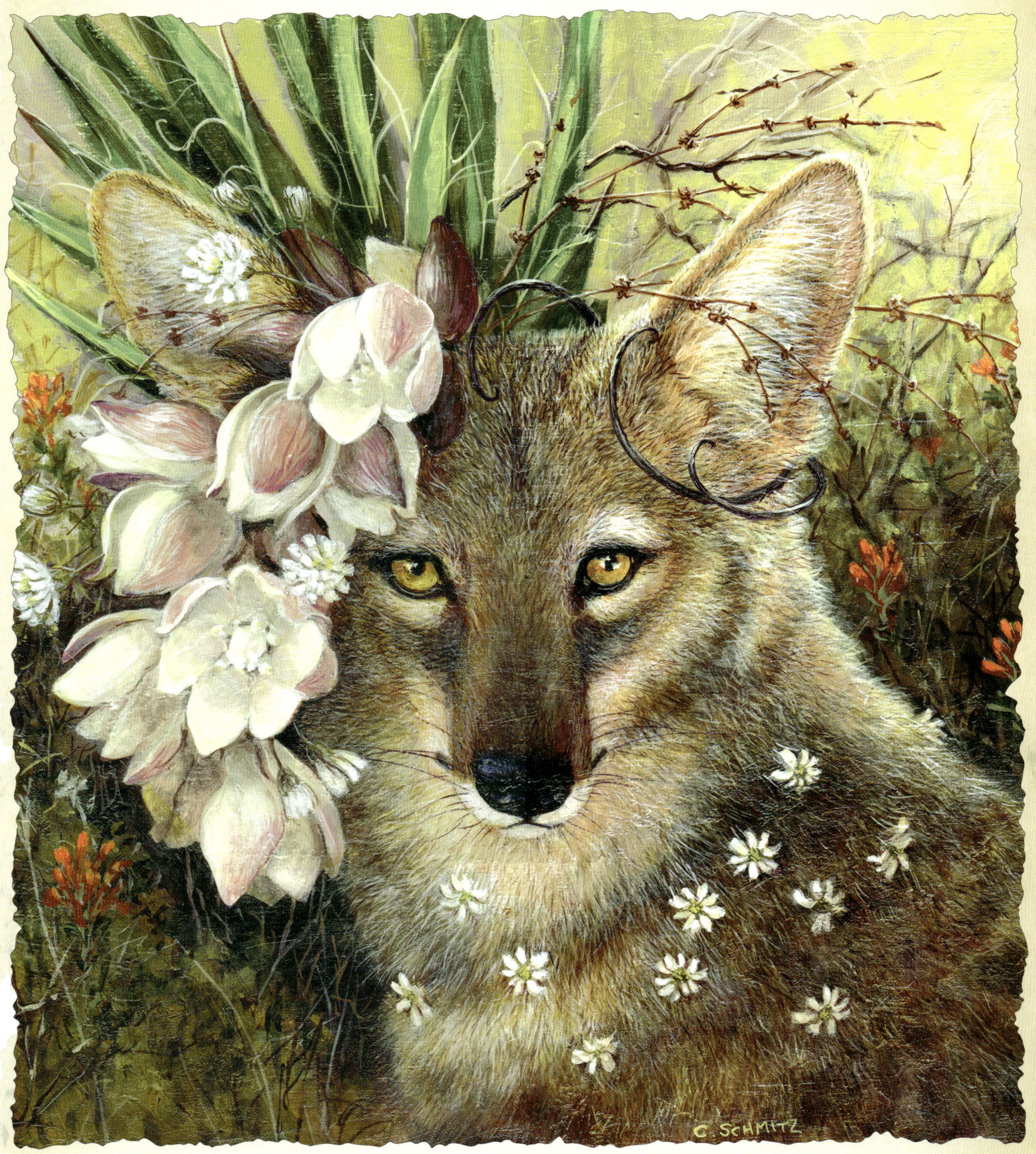
C. SCHMITZ

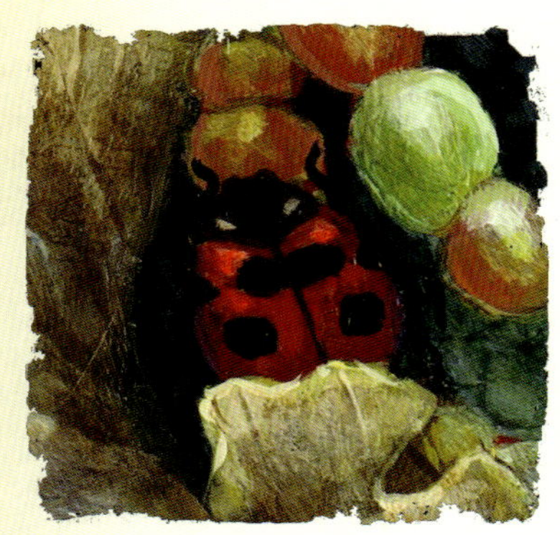

A dapper collared lizard showed off how he used small findings for big impact. A Mojave aster, desert checkerspot wing, lilac sunbonnet leaves, monkeyflower, and a rare pygmy poppy tilted precariously on his head. The tail of a giant hairy scorpion was proof of his courage. Around his neck swirled pods and petals of Eureka Dunes evening primrose. A strand of iodine bush stems was clasped with a compliant ladybug.

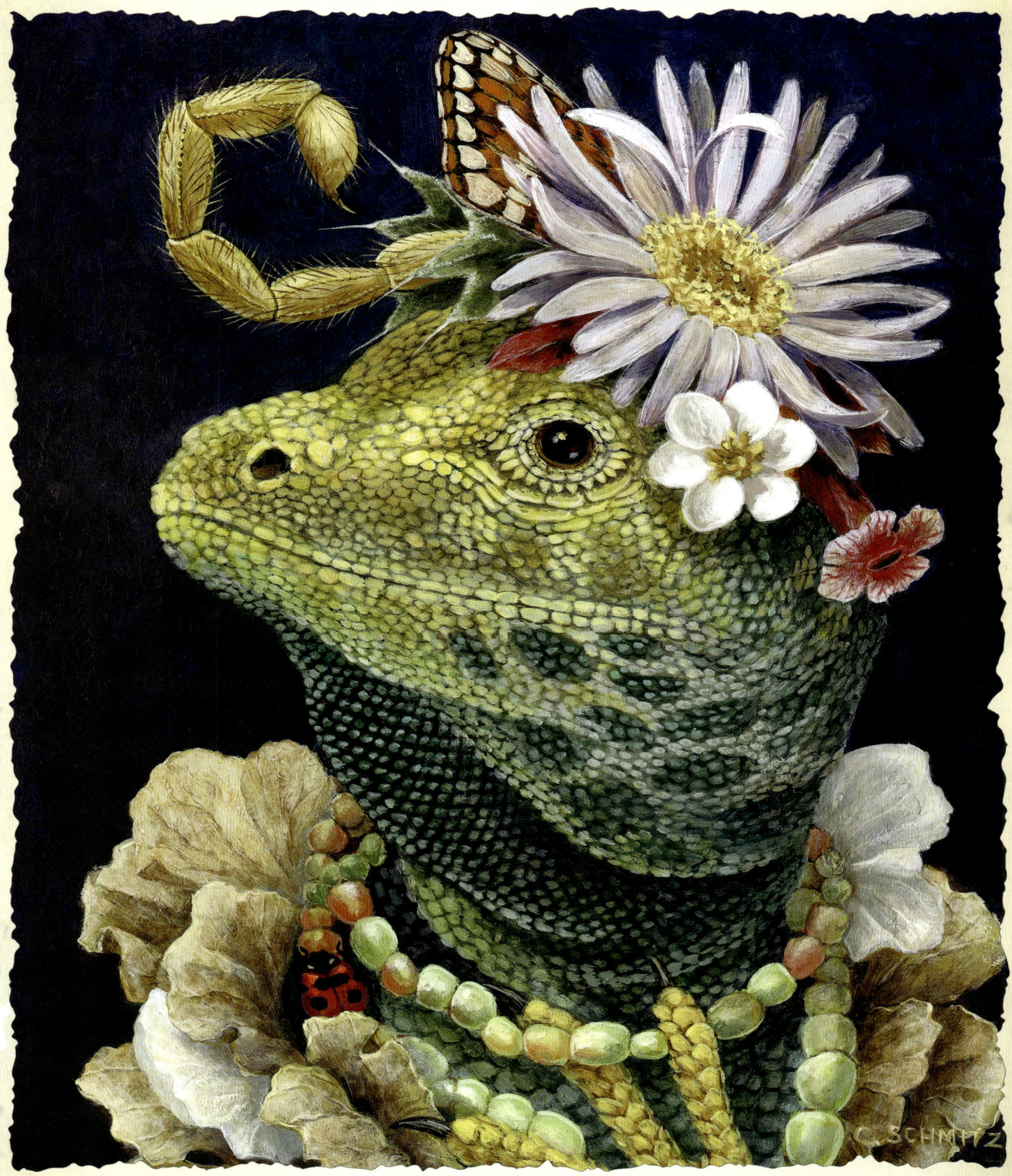
C. SCHMITZ

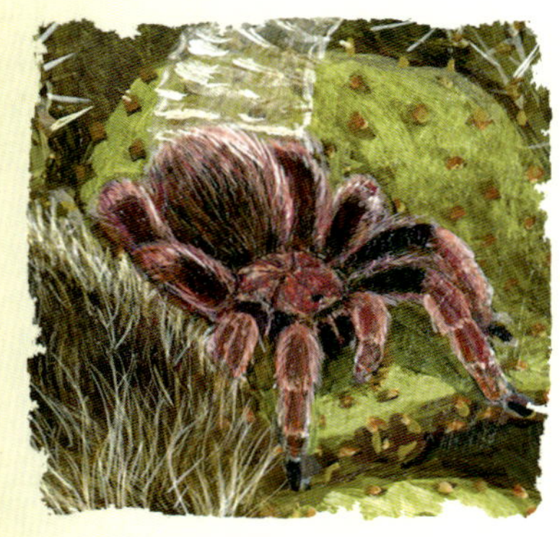

A javelina trotted in, bursting with wild textures and vibrant colors—cholla, mammillaria, prickly pear cacti, snakeskins, fairy duster, creosote seeds and, suspended from a devil's claw, a rattlesnake rattle!

"What did that cost her?" snipped a cactus mouse. "And how did she get that Mexican pink tarantula?"

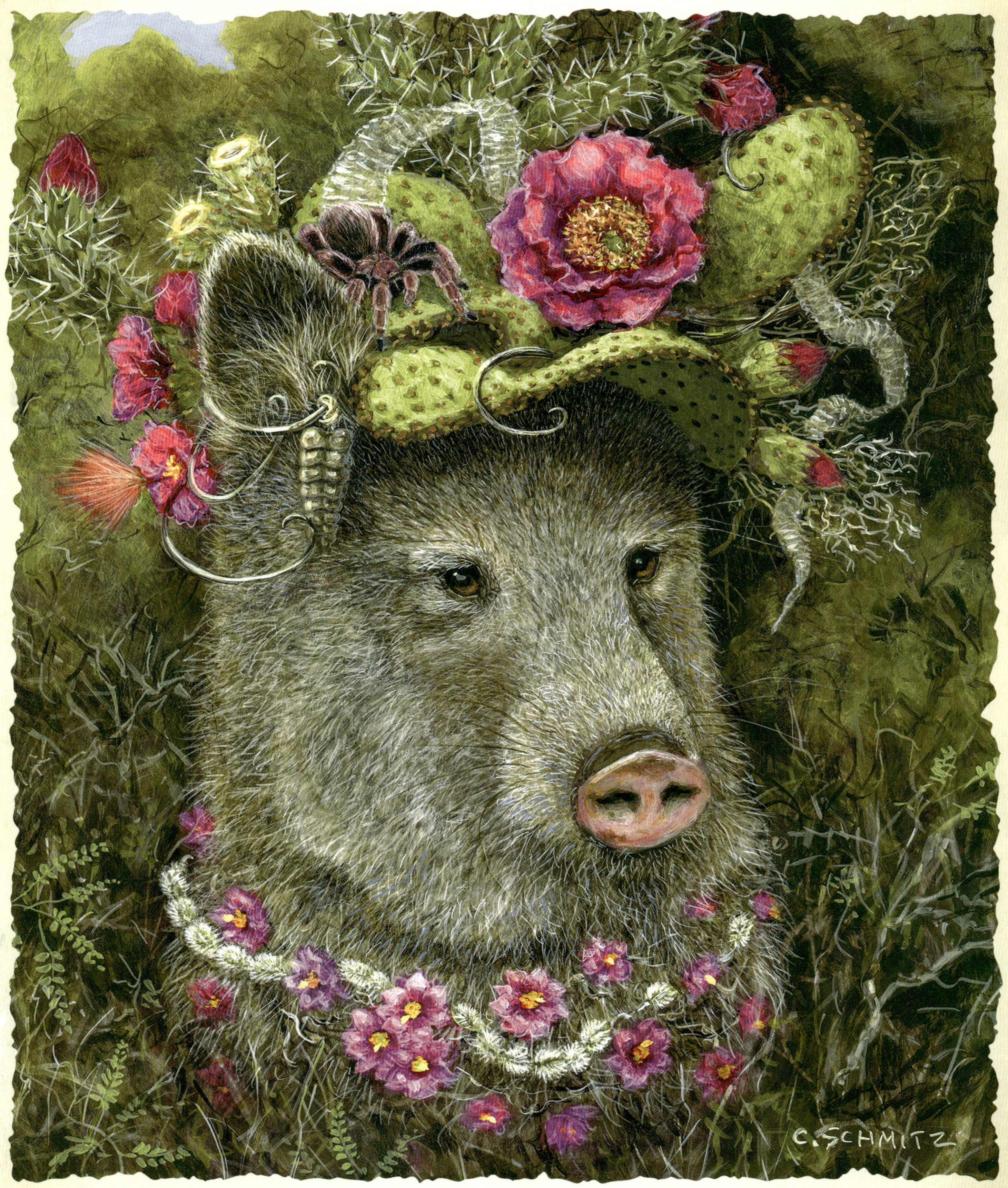
C. SCHMITZ

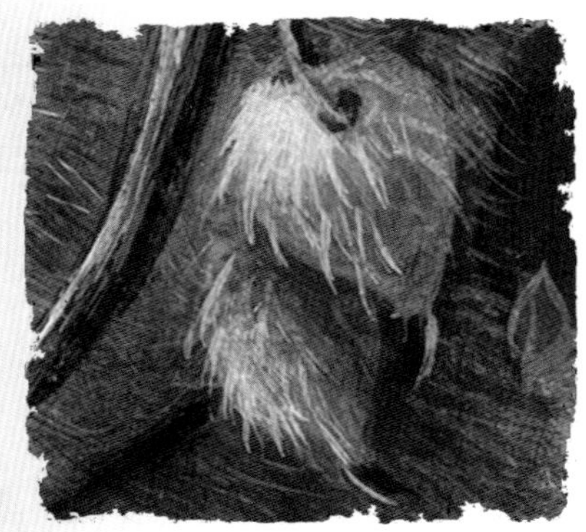

Most eager to dress up were the ground squirrels, always far too busy in their khaki overalls to even consider such frivolity. One working girl became a lady of breeding in her dotted green beret with lush Apache plumes and a flourish of mesquite leaves. Devil's claws held the cactus pad in place.

Stingers and segments of scorpion tails made earrings and a necklace. Rattlesnake weed, with its miniature jewel-like flowers, slipped seductively from her shoulders.

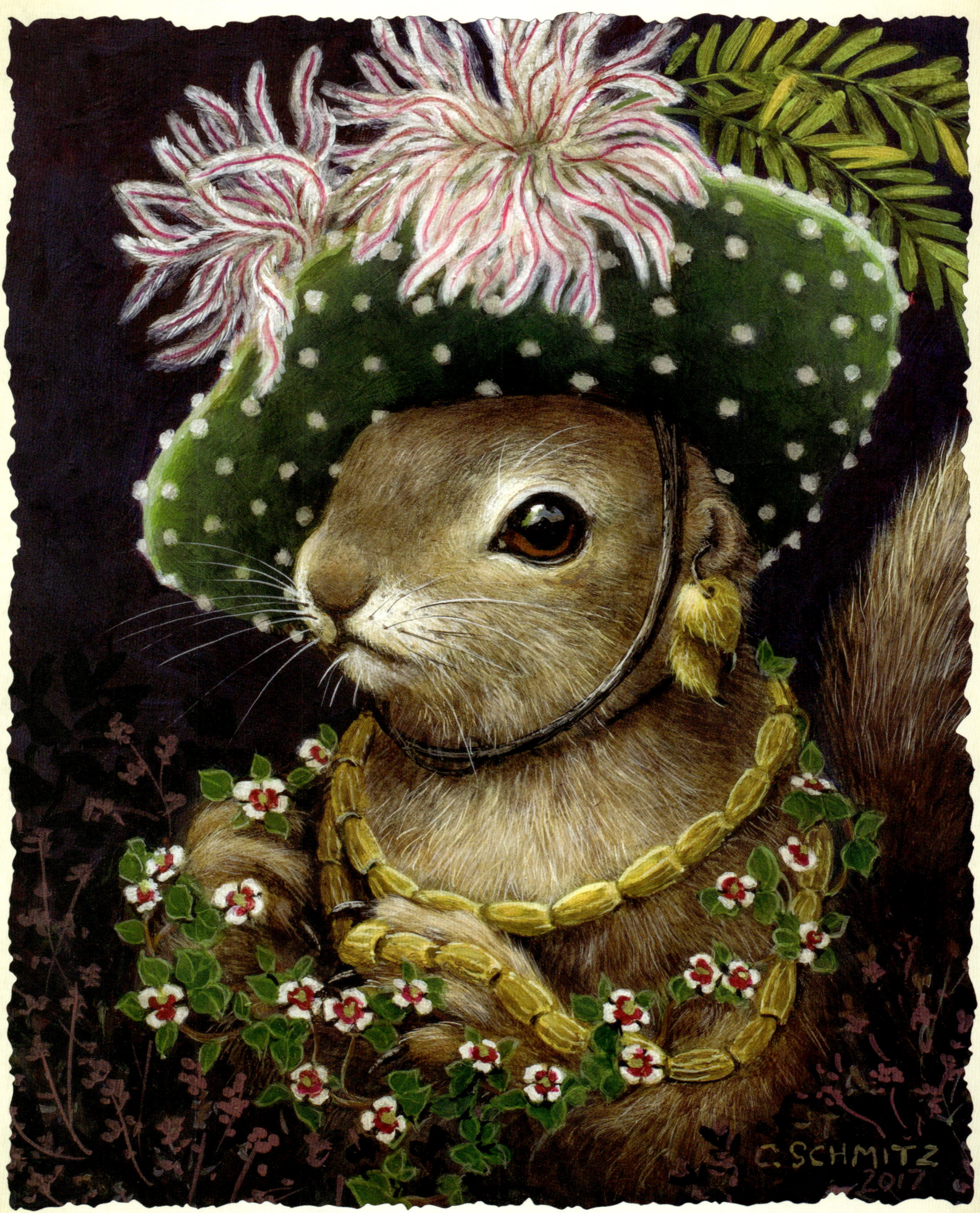
C. SCHMITZ
2017

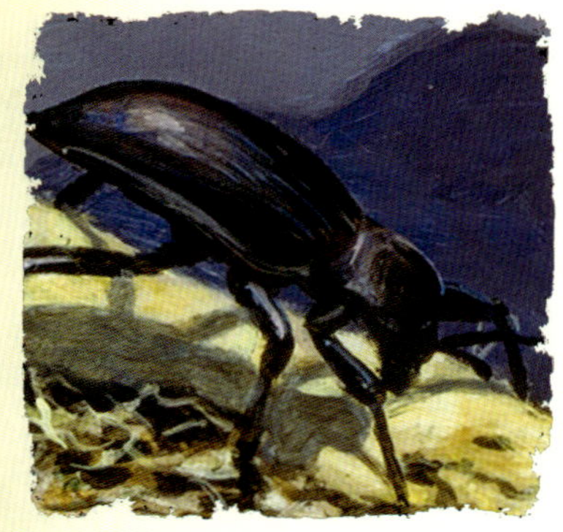

A coati mundi ran into a darkling beetle while out nosing around.

"You smell weird," he snorted.

"Are you a clown?" retorted the bug, eyeing the shabby fedora with its odd assortment of fetishes.

They immediately became friends. The beetle climbed aboard among cactus fiber, devil's claw, fairy duster, screwbean mesquite, datura pods, a nopalito, and a Vermilion Flycatcher's feather. They set out for the Wild Hat Celebration, gathering wildflowers along the way. Milkweed, globemallow, acacia, salvia, palo verde, Tahoka daisies, desert phlox, broom dalea, and tufted grasses made ideal tokens of good will.

"We also brought along a sprig of allthorn. In case somebody needs a little jab."

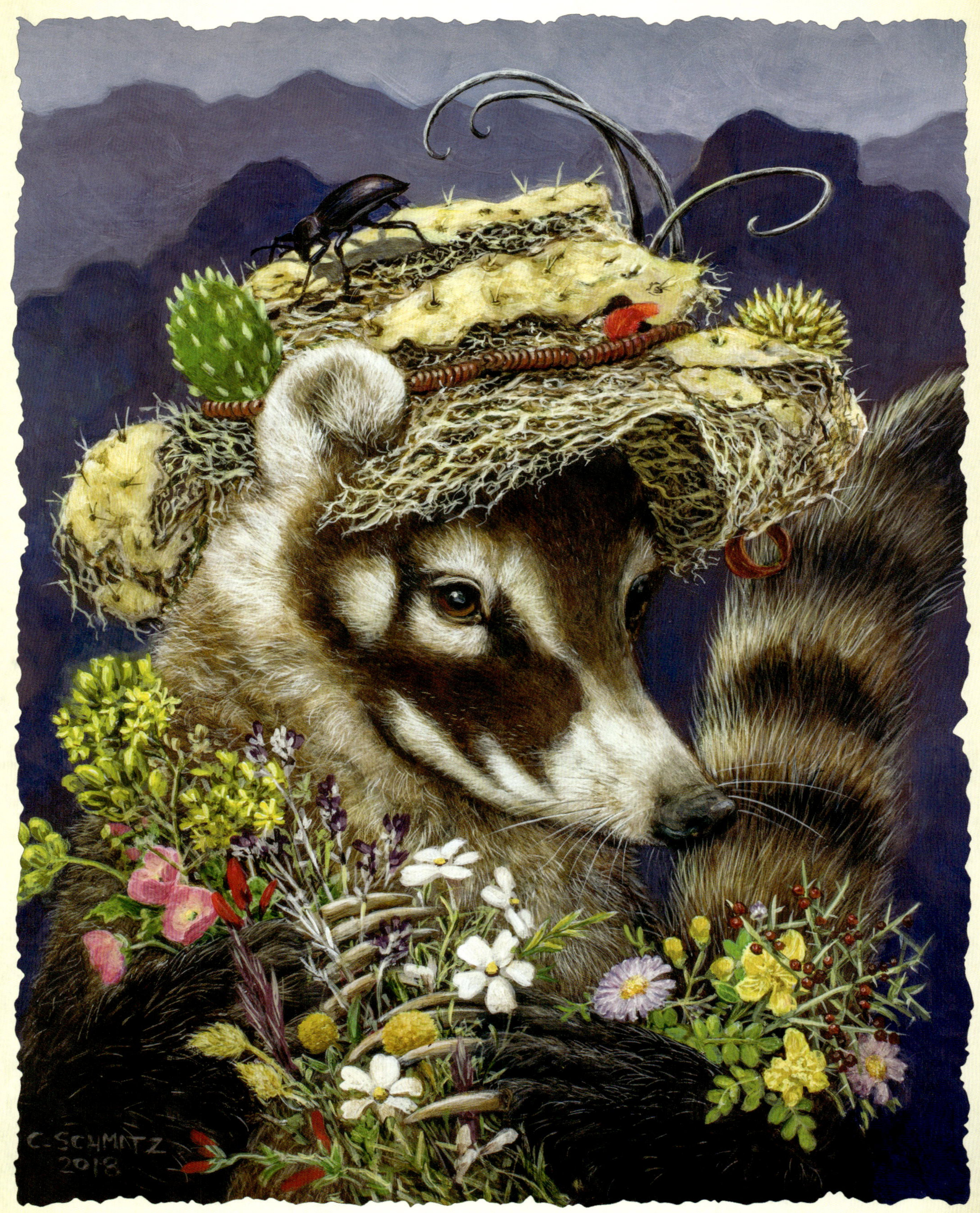
C. SCHMATZ
2018

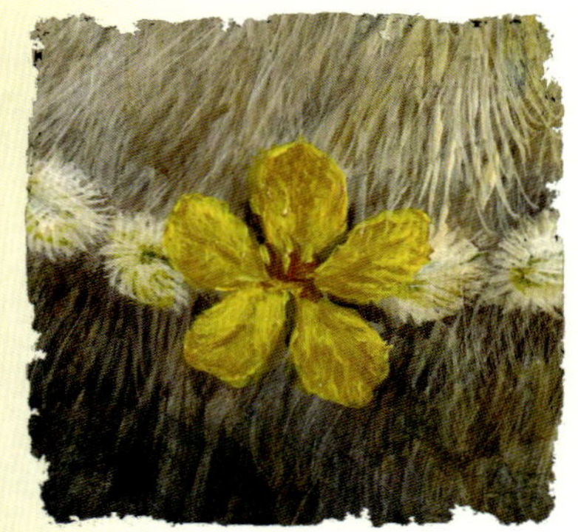

Scantily shaded under a brim of cactus fiber, a bobcat politely mingled with the other contestants. Puffy blooms of acacia, desert fern, fairy duster, and Apache plume were spaced around a sunny prickly pear flower pinned with a devil's claw. A bud and fruit made a drop earring, a sotol leaf held a plus-size snakeskin bow, and a senna flower rested on a string of creosote seeds. Glancing around at the number of prey animals, she was sure that other bobcats would show up.

"I'll have someone to flirt with!"

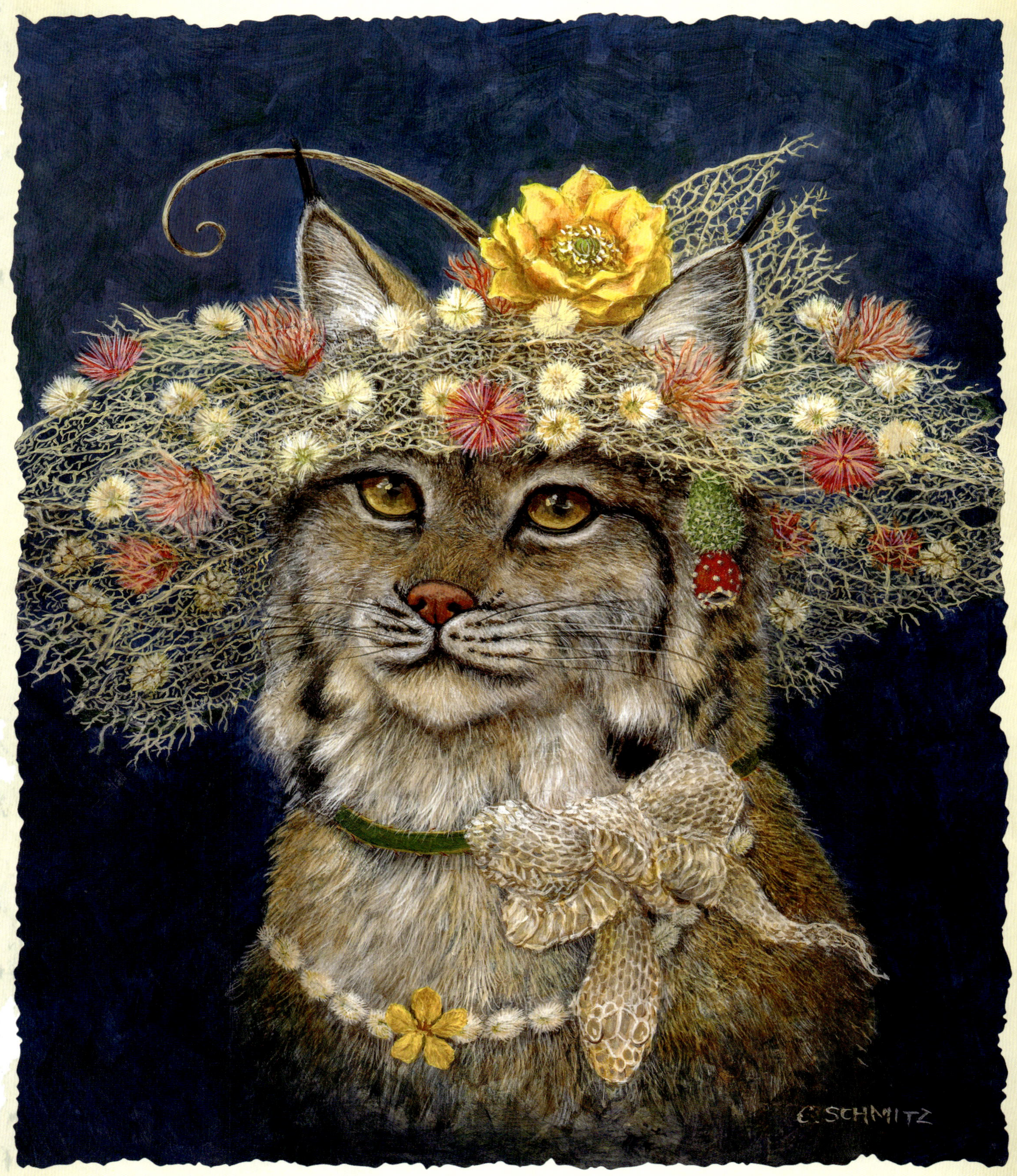
C. SCHMITZ

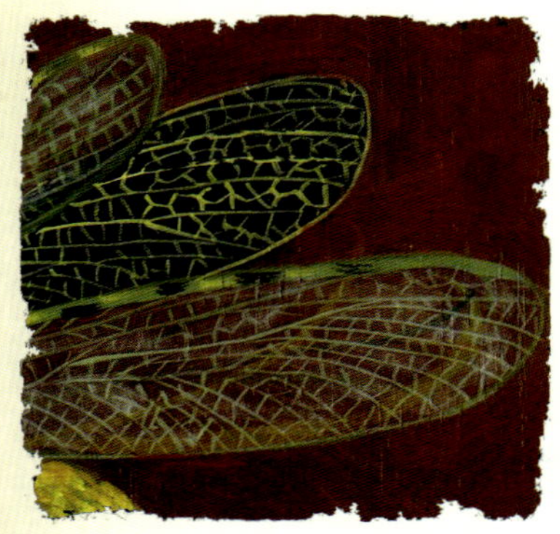

In the milling crowd, another collared lizard protected his best friend, a cheeky kangaroo rat. She wore a globemallow blossom with a mist of ricegrass, while he sported a bibelot of blister beetle legs and antennae, grasshopper wings, and velvet ant parts.

"My manly millipede necklace is not for the ticklish!" he bragged.

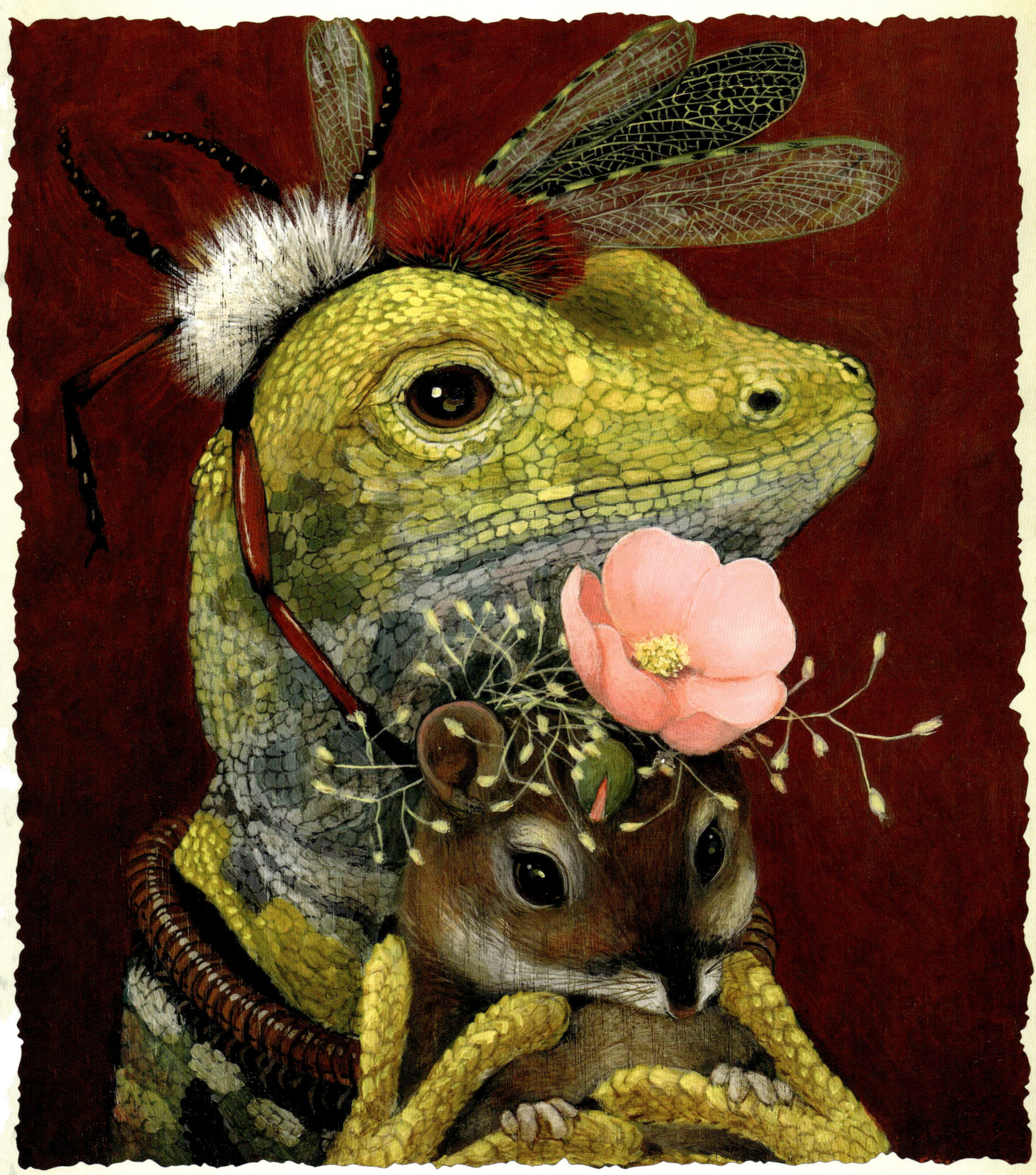

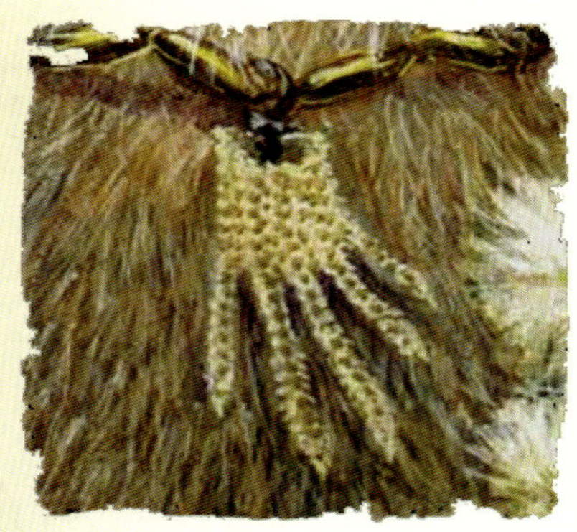

Timidly waiting in the creosote, a jackrabbit marveled at such variety. Cactus fiber and devil's claw, always popular, formed her airy crest dotted with desert fern blossoms and itty-bitty mammillaria cactus flowers. Creosote seeds and acacia blossoms draped over her shoulders.

She noted with satisfaction, however, that one of her pieces was unique. From a choker of June beetle legs hung a rare charm—the glove-like skin of a lizard's dainty hand, magically left intact when he had slipped it off.

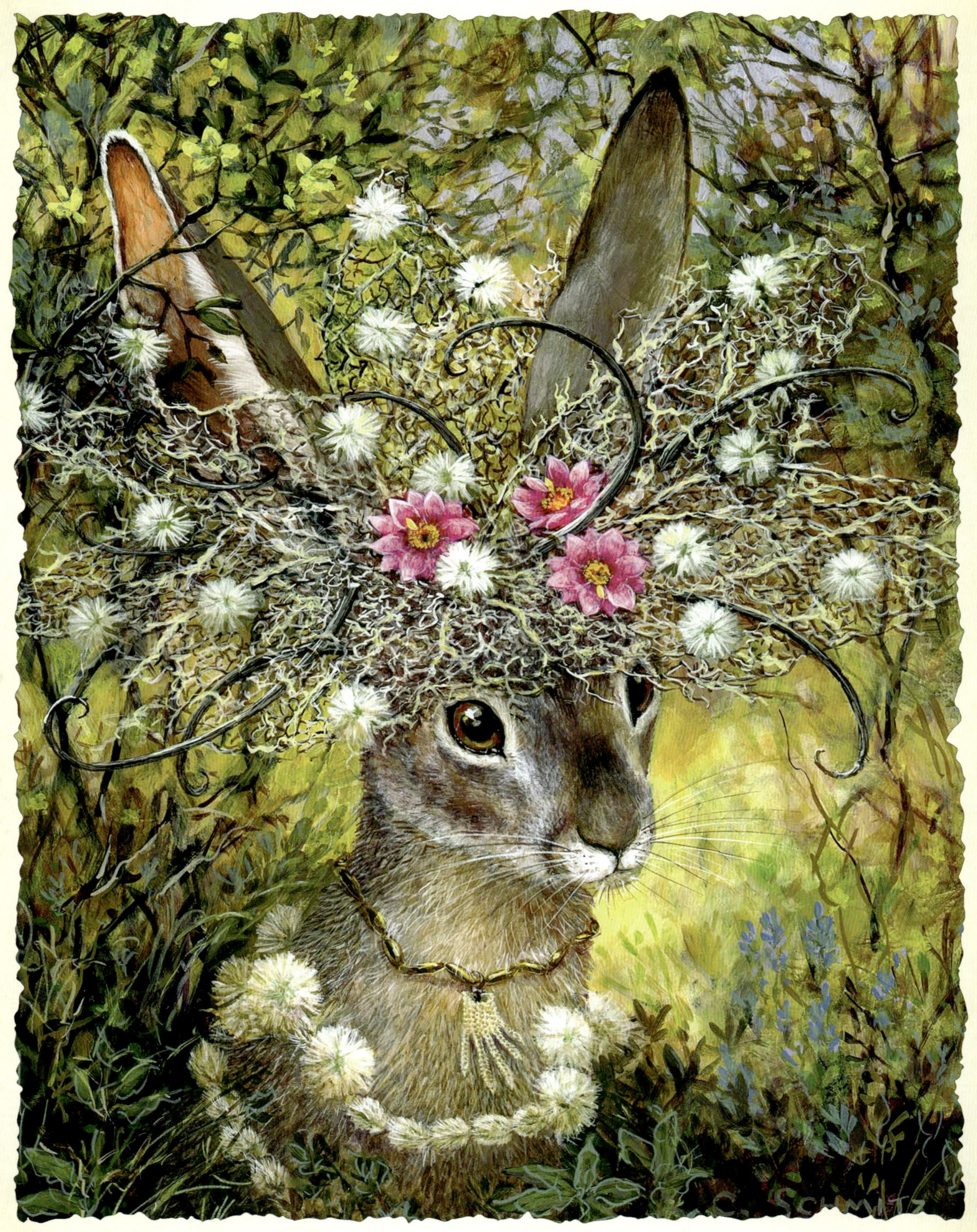

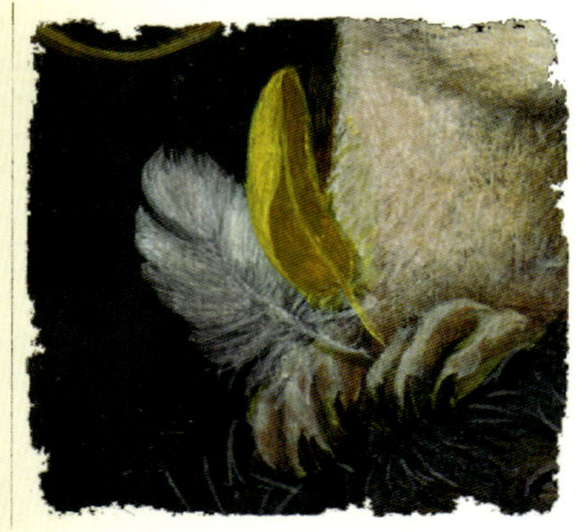

A smartly dressed skunk ambled down from the high country. Lacking dexterity in her bear-like paws, she had recruited her chipmunk pal. He formed a velvety toque from a common mullein leaf, then spiked it with grape vines, Arizona cudweed, and rare curly ponderosa pine needles.

"For a breath of magenta I used fetid goosefoot," he chirped. "It forms a pink haze over the forest floor in the fall. Oak galls and juniper berries made super baubles."

Everyone gushed over the skunk's hat and sensuous tail, lest she make a stink.

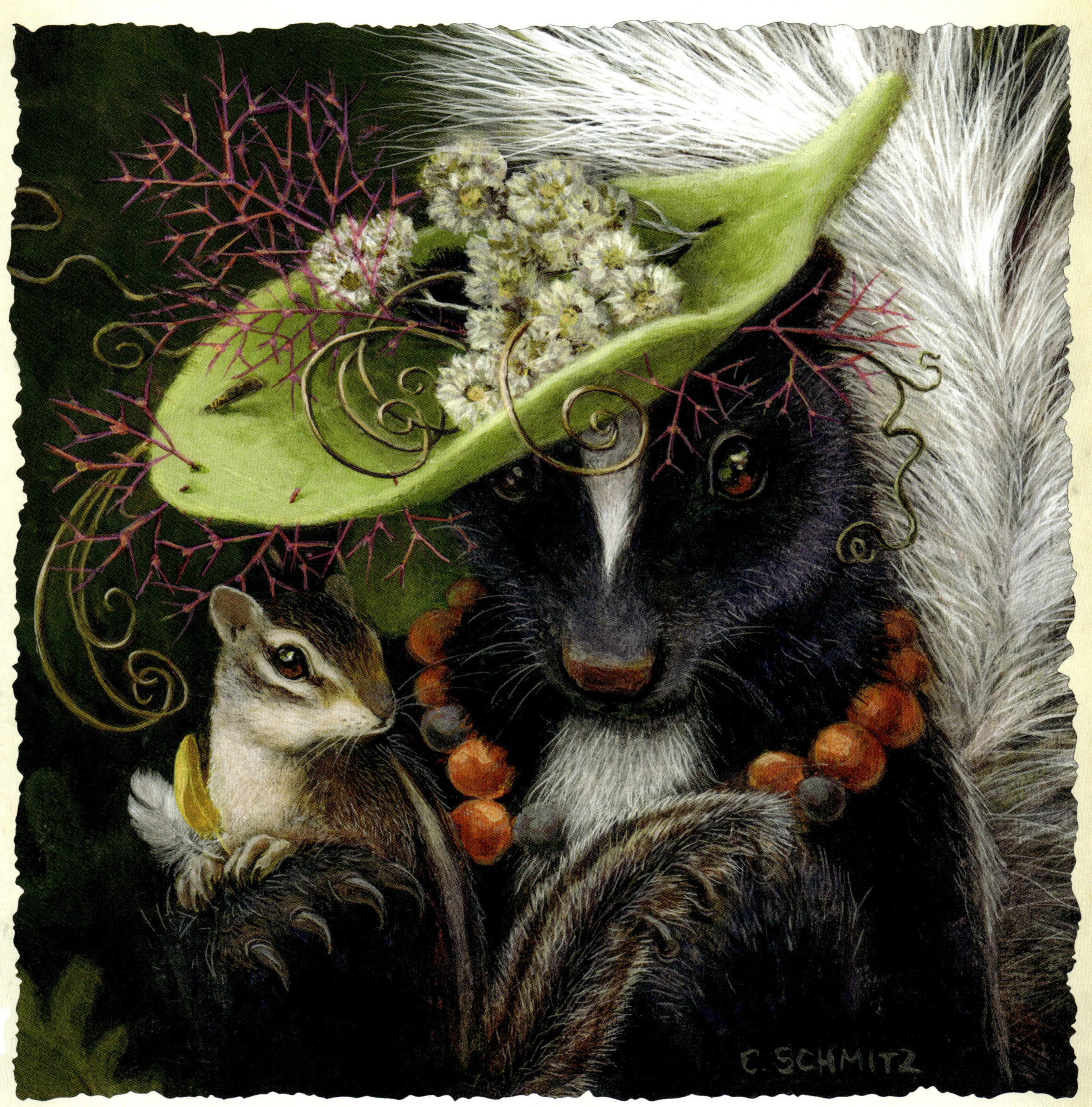
C. SCHMITZ

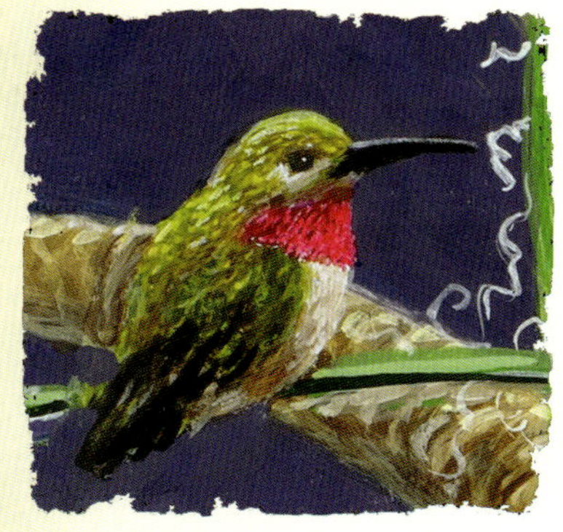

A young ewe of the bighorn family often felt invisible. Plain and tan, with bare slivers of horn, she faded easily into the canyon walls. But not today! She skipped from rock to rock, down the mountain to the Wild Hat Competition.

"Rams get all the attention for wearing bulky crash helmets," she had complained to the orioles who were crafting her hat. "Make me into a shooting star!"

Desert paintbrush sizzled at the tips of red yucca leaves; desert fern, spreading daisies and a globemallow orbited around her face and neck. Fine filigrees of dried grama grass scrolled like music. Buzzing close by was a shimmering hummingbird.

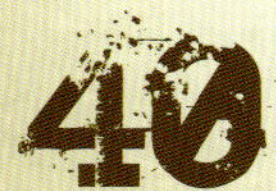

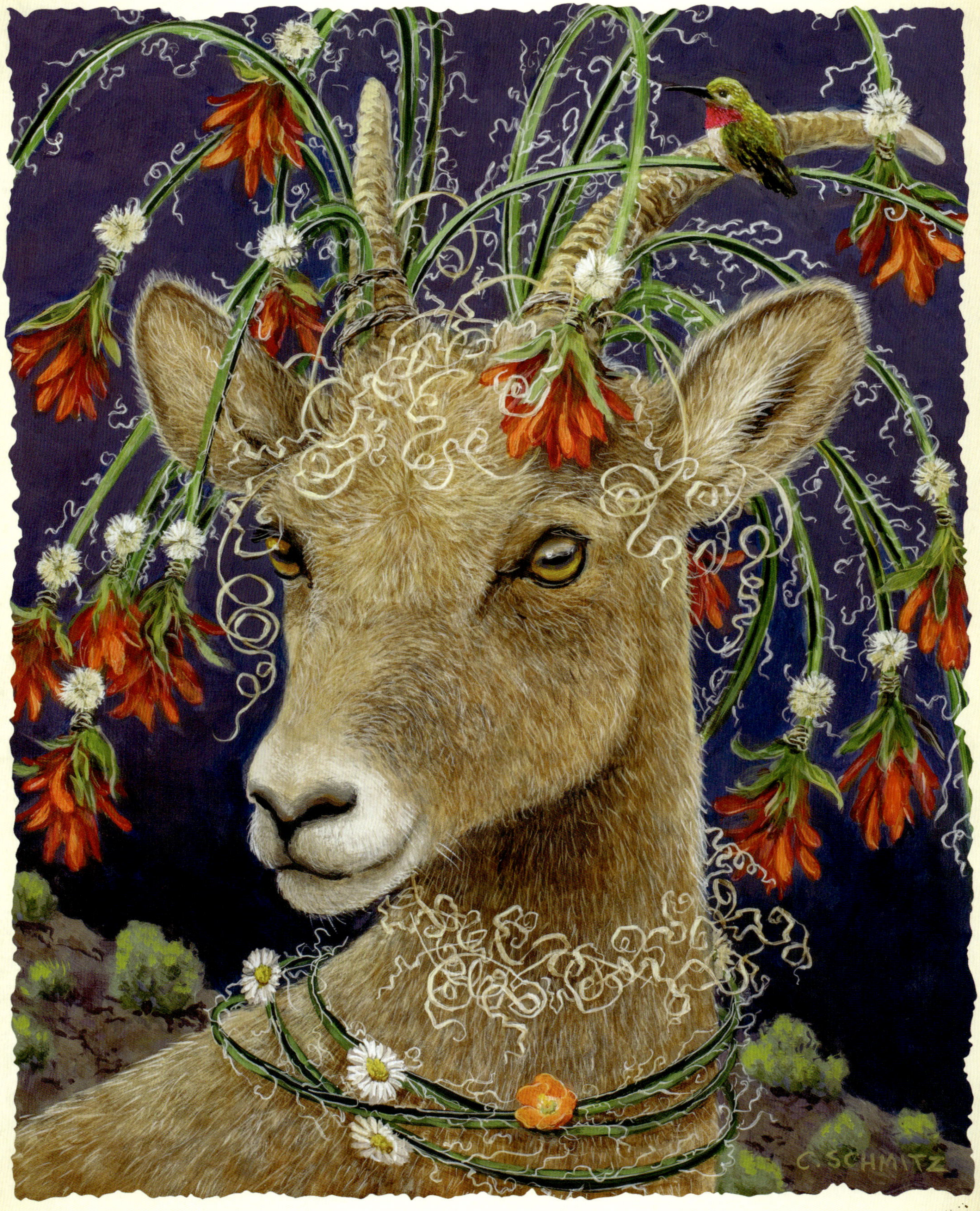

A cougar chose vibrant hues of red to attract attention. An array of ocotillo, cholla, hedgehog cacti, chuparosa, fairy duster, and coral bean blossoms were anchored to one ear by a devil's claw. Ladybugs, scorpion tails, and cactus fruits made a seductive neck piece. A barrel cactus spine, piercing his ear, hinted of danger.

Several rabbits exchanged nervous squeaks upon the arrival of the bobcat and the cougar.

"Why were the cats invited?"

"What if they had NOT been invited?" said an owl.

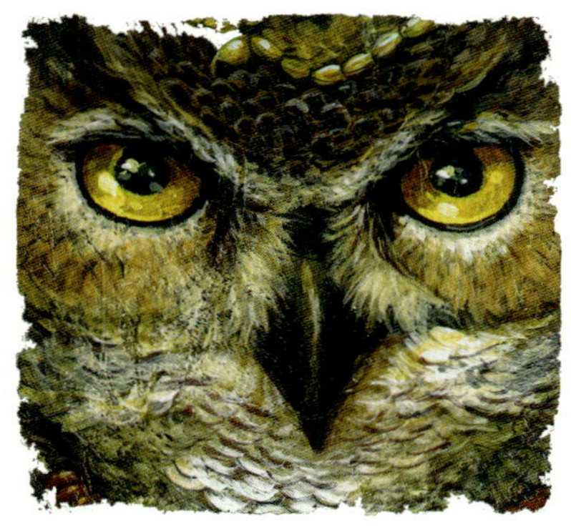

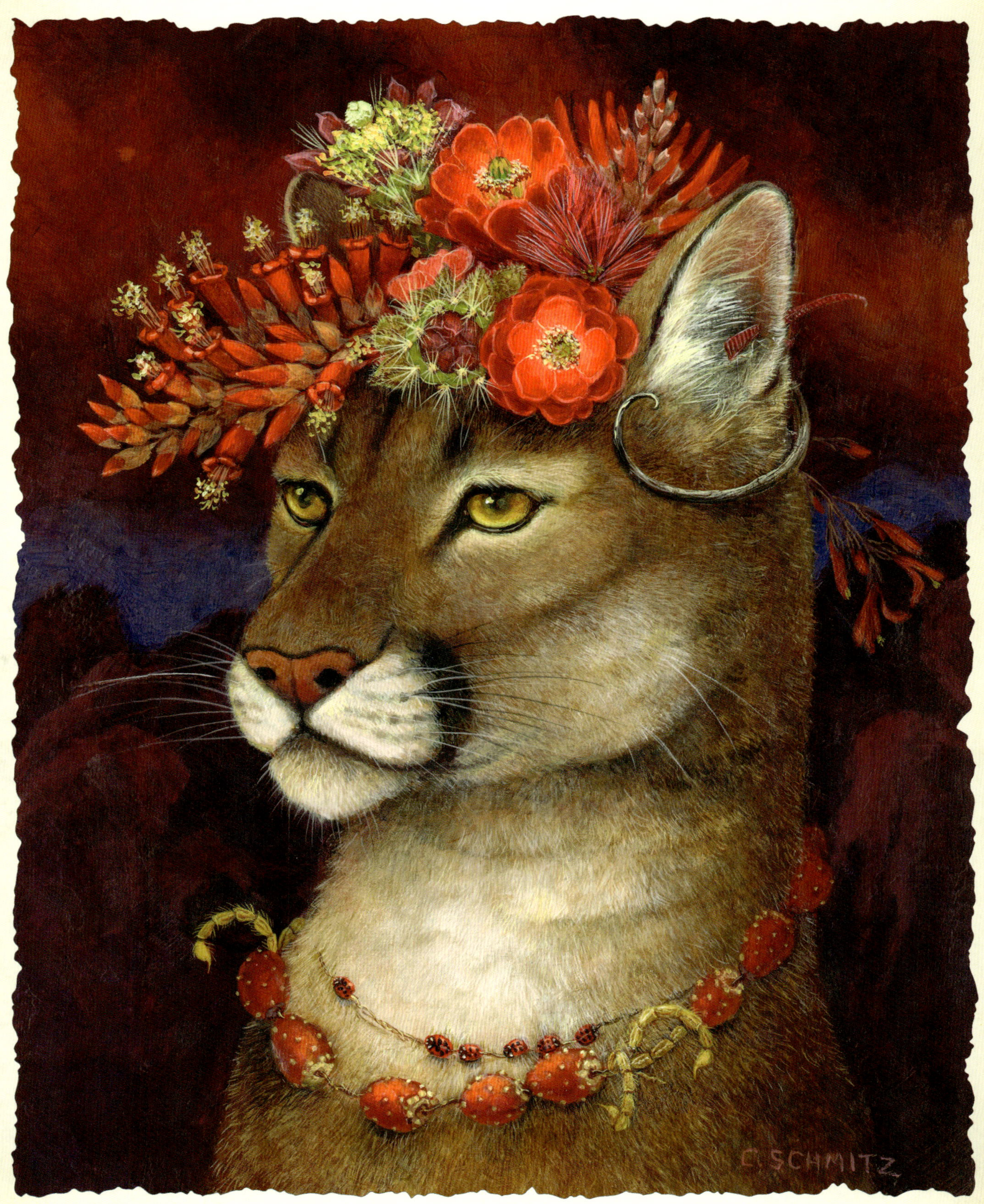
C. SCHMITZ

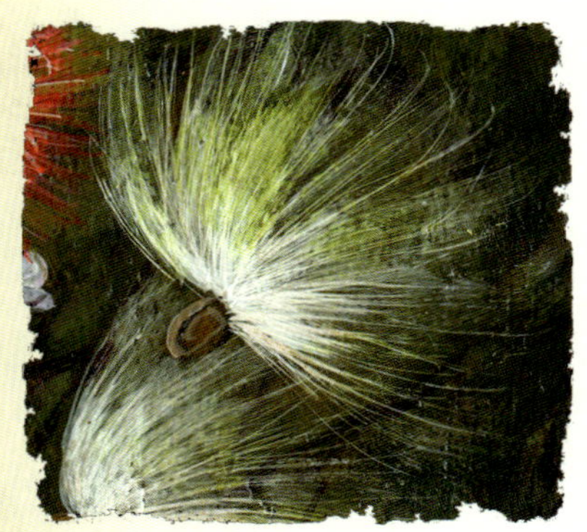

Sheltered by a thicket of thorns, a desert cottontail gazed up at the flowering canopy far beyond her reach. A Cactus Wren noticed her wistful expression.

"Another bunny with spring fever," he sighed as he began tossing down fluffy, confetti-colored blossoms for her—acacia, mesquite, desert fern, velvetpod mimosa, plume tiquilia, and Baja red fairy duster. For jewelry, they found a scorpion tail and creosote seeds, then set to work. The rabbit soon cuddled in luxury as seeds from a milkweed pod pirouetted up and away in the breeze.

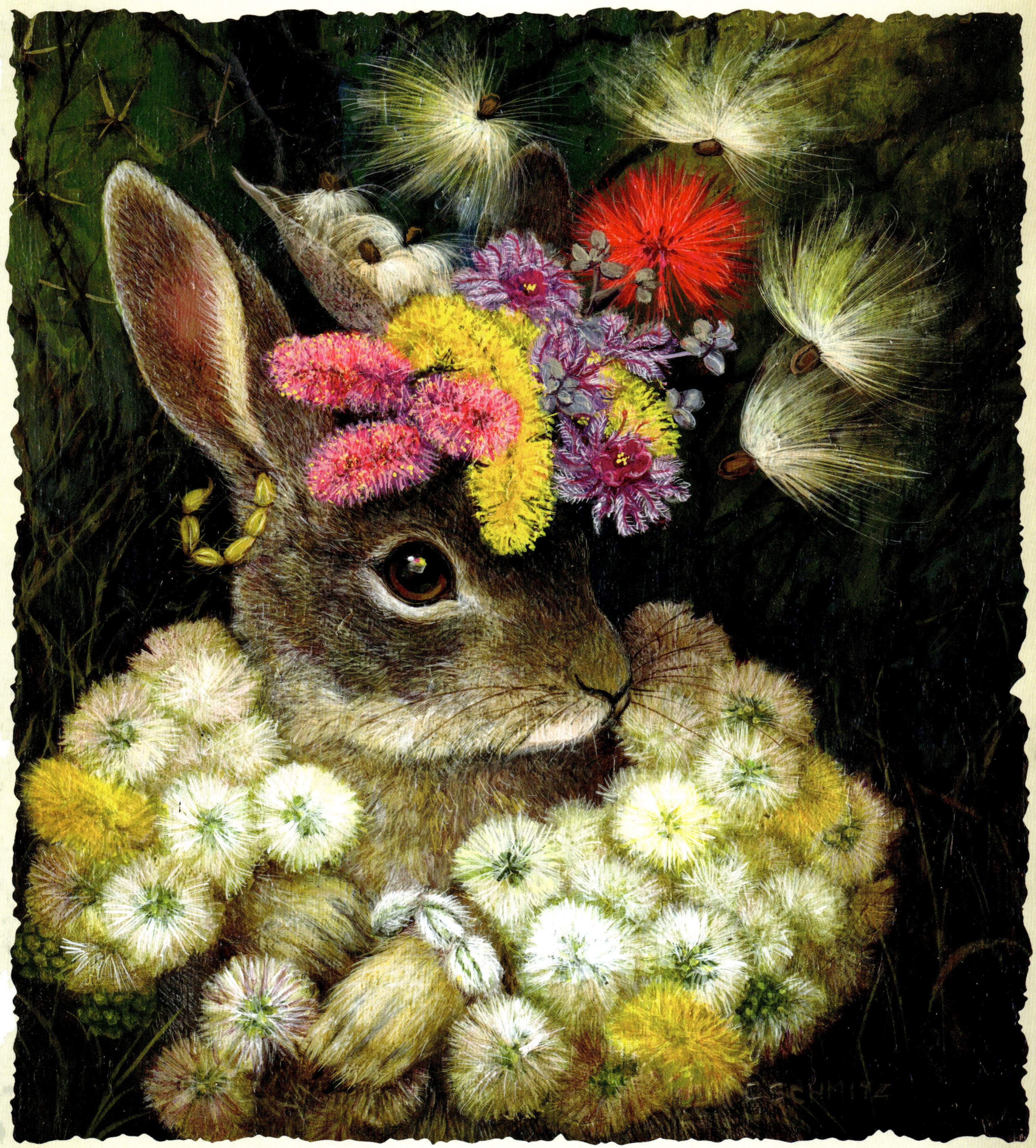

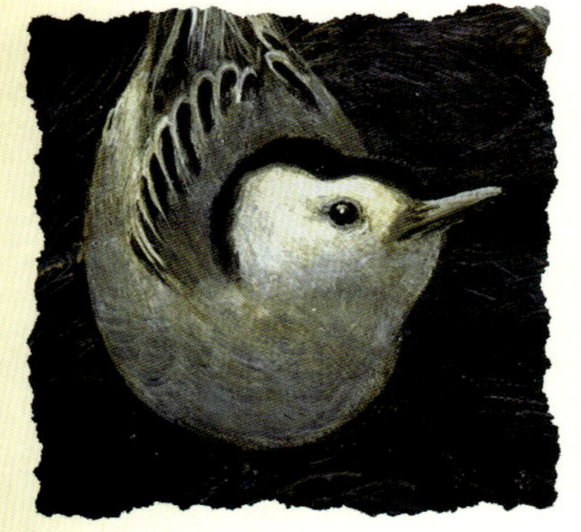

A current of apprehension passed through the crowd as a dark, formidable figure loomed into view. Most of them had never seen a black bear. Anxiety gave way to admiration as she eased into a comfortable pose with her avian companions and began to chat.

"Rumors of a shindig reached the foothills and then the mountains," she told them. "We found the idea absurd. We just had to come!"

Her leafy headdress trembled as a Blue Grosbeak fiddled with an arrangement of aspen, mullein, Gambel oak, and sprays of pine needles. Twists of grape vine and oak galls formed her necklace and earring. A White-breasted Nuthatch and a Pygmy Nuthatch twittered with a Green-tailed Towhee.

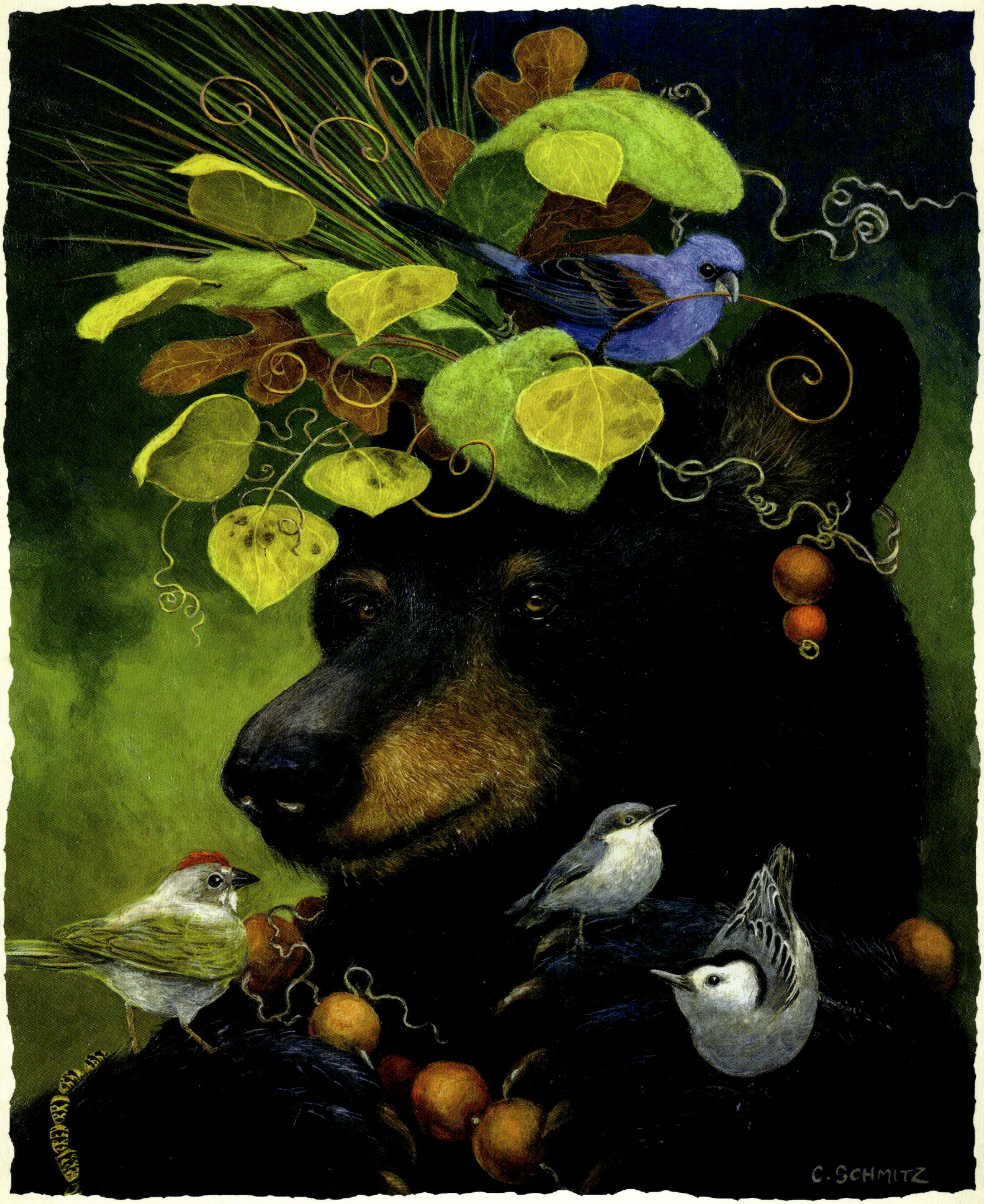

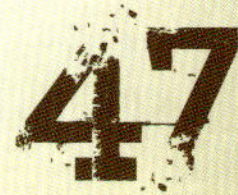

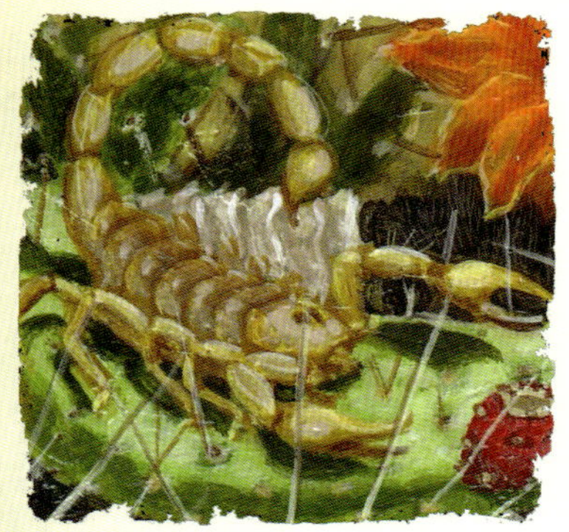

An armada of needles and explosive color maneuvered slowly through the brittlebush. Barely visible under interlocking branches of cholla was a javelina. Two well-groomed coyotes rolled their eyes. Scraps of snakeskin, yucca, cactus fruits, globemallow, devil's claw, and a siren bloom from a barrel cactus were caught among the spines. A fat scorpion, coaxed onto a prickly pear pad, struck a classic pose. Creosote seeds, desert fern, and scorpion tails edged the javelina's natural collar.

The coyotes howled with laughter.

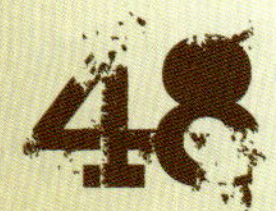

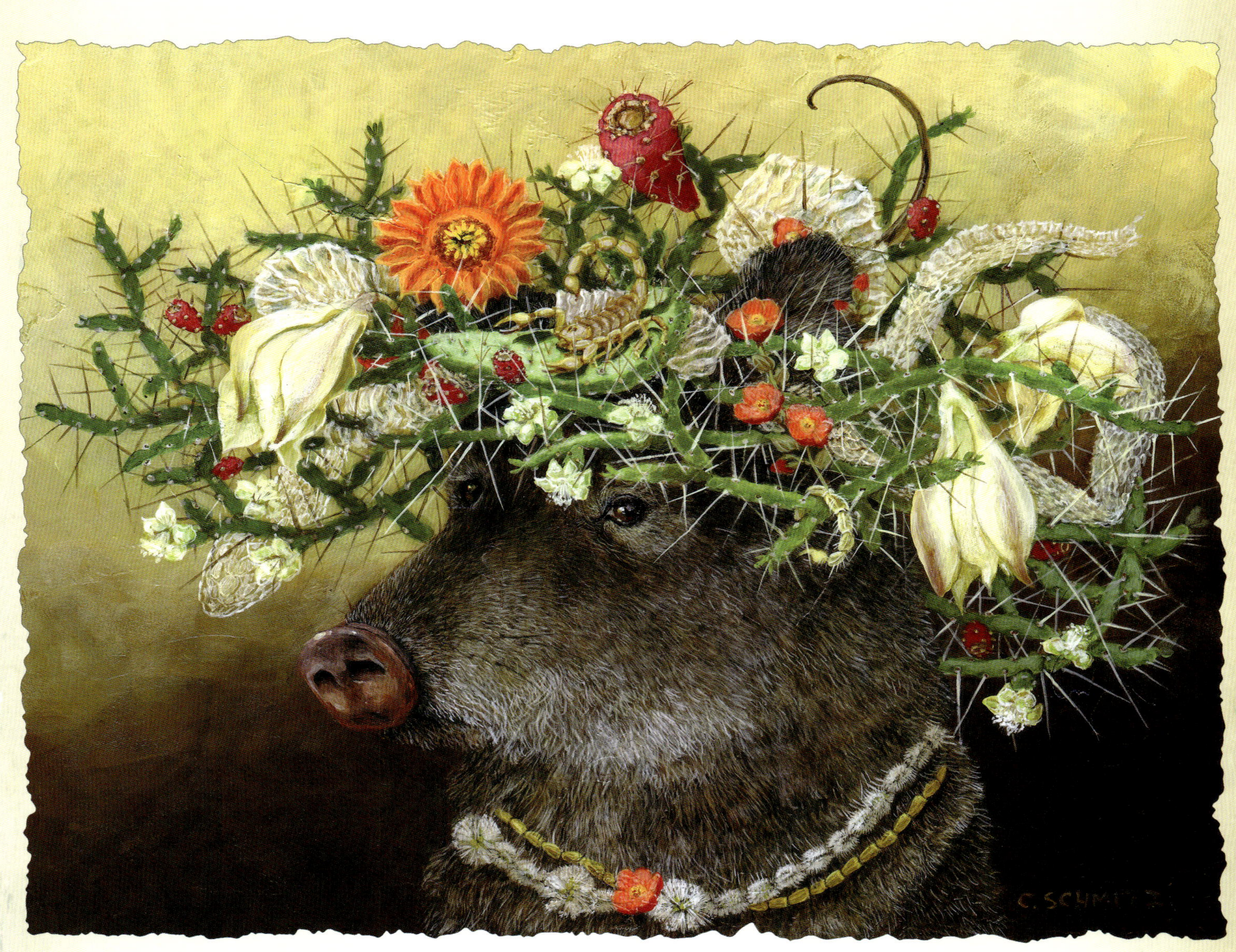
C. SCHMITZ

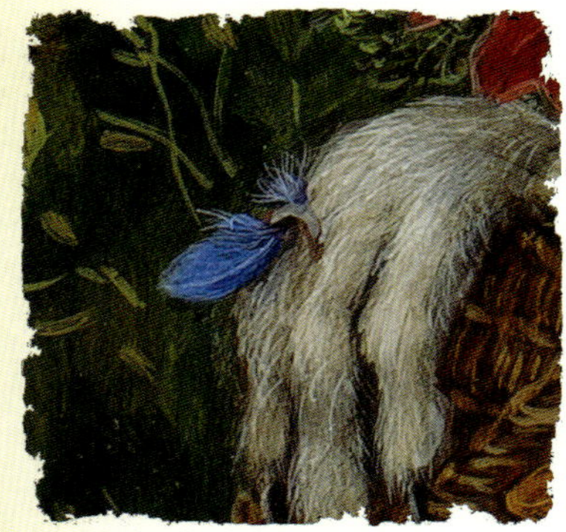

Ruffled leaves of wild geranium and silvery wands of mountain mahogany seeds made a dream outfit for an Abert's tassel-eared squirrel.

"I made it myself," she said. "I stuffed bunches of lichen here and there because it reminded me of shredded patio pillows."

Curly needles of ponderosa pine were secured with grape vines. Feathers from a woodpecker's cap looked like tiny flames at the tips of her ears. (To avoid a kerfuffle, a Scrub Jay simply donated one of his.) A satchel woven from pine needles and tough grasses with a leathery oak leaf applique held precision tools she had taken from a jeweler's shop.

"No problem getting in there!" she giggled. "But I eschewed acorn jewelry. Please. I found GOLD—the gleaming thighs of June beetles!"

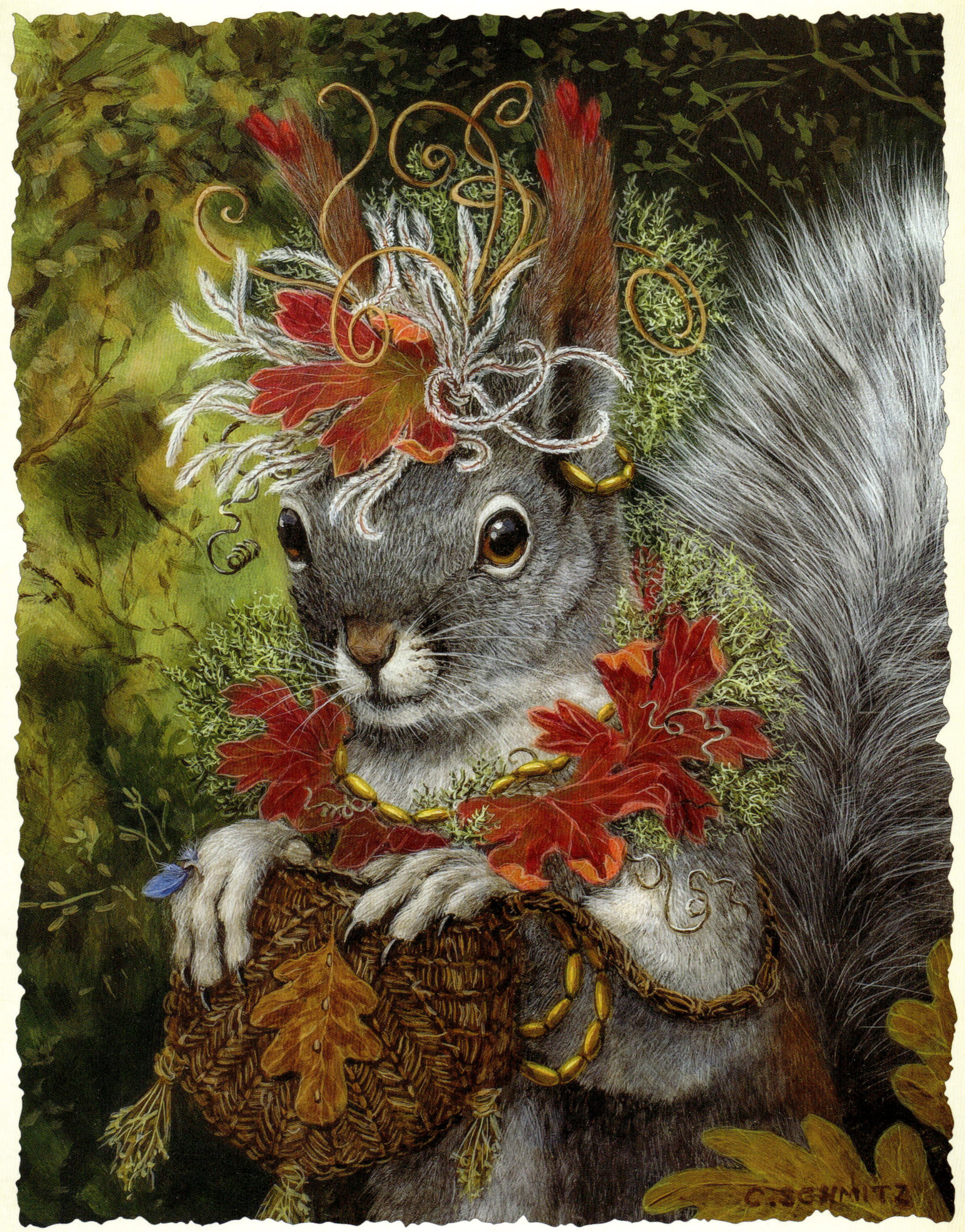
C. SCHMITZ

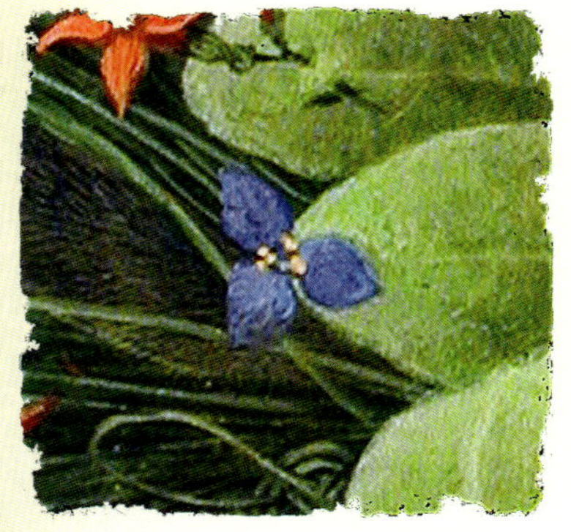

A bobcat, identified by his tufted ears and luxurious chops, was more than pleased with his forest topknot—as compensation for his short tail, perhaps. Overlapping mullein leaves sprung from a headband of macramé pine needles. One silvery townsendia daisy, a western dayflower, and arcs of scarlet gilia would have been enough.

"But how could I NOT tuck in a couple of rabbit ears?" he mused. "And their cottony tails looked so nice with the pussy willows."

The anxious rabbits dared not ask the bobcat for an apology. Nevertheless, they controlled their urge to panic after reassuring gestures from the bears and the skunks.

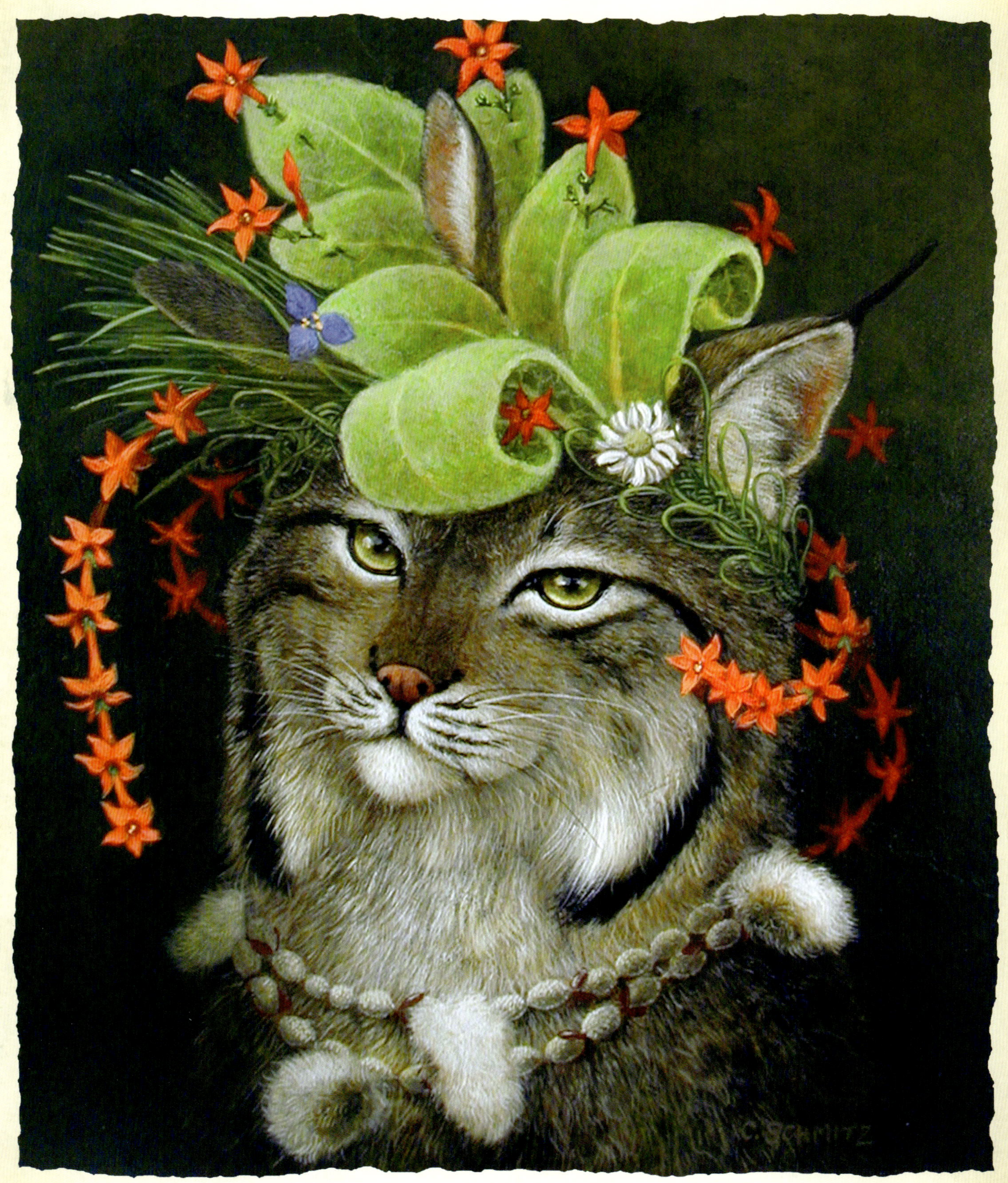
C. SCHMITZ

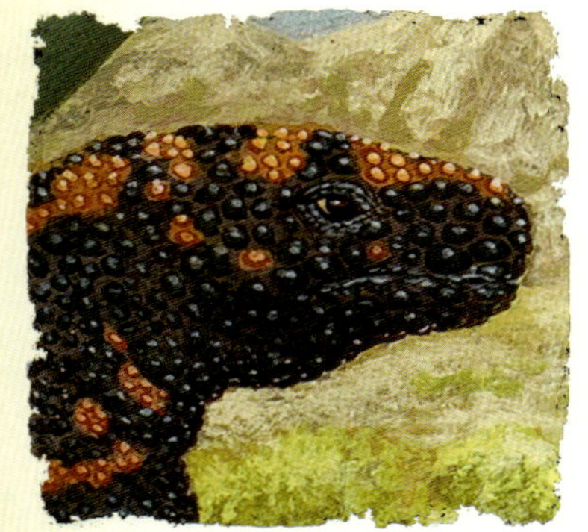

The hubbub suddenly stopped. Hushed with wonder, the animals gathered around a rock shelf. There, like a glowing ember, was a tiny, twirling figure—a Gila monster up on her toes! Everyone was mesmerized, never having seen the underside of a Gila monster at all, and surely not a dancing one.

"At least she's wearing something," snarked the skink.

Apache plumes and prickly poppy petals fluttered in a skirt of cactus fiber, dotted with flicker feathers, acacia, palo verde, shrubby dogweed, and desert fern blossoms. Snake rattles, scorpion tails, a sprig of cane beardgrass, rattlesnake weed, and a snakeskin scarf wafted as she turned.

A chuckwalla, flattening herself into a crevice, watched with one eye. "Shameless! That undulating inner-tube is no dancer."

A spiny lizard in sparkling armor was enthralled. "What a pair we'd make!"

A young Gila gent, handsome in tight leather studded with copper and carbon, breathed, "I must have her!"

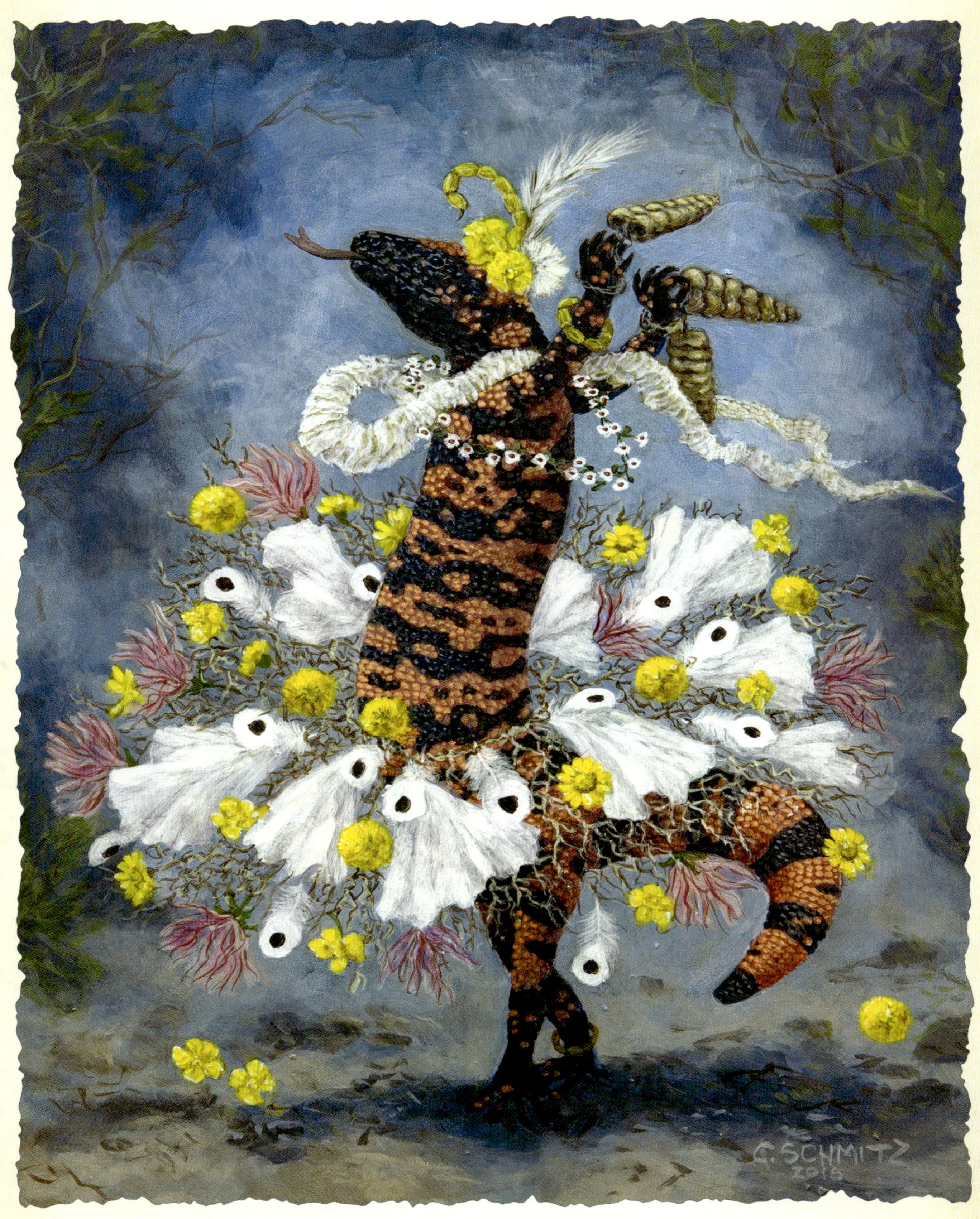
G. SCHMITZ

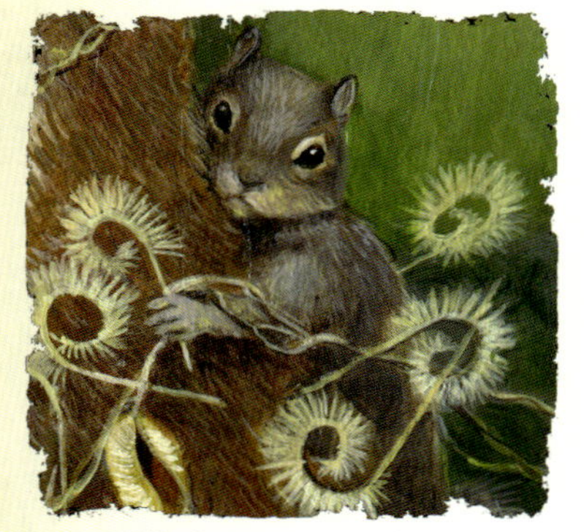

Just when they thought they'd seen it all, a pronghorn antelope crowned with soaring antlers and grassland flora strutted in. Several javelina girls swooned. Wild buckwheat, grama grass, hesperaloe pods, and devil's claws were secured to his antlers with needle and thread grass by a Vermilion Flycatcher.

A ground squirrel straddled his neck like a mini-jockey, clutching a strand of Tahoka daisies, scarlet gilia, and grama grass. A bell-like yucca blossom swayed at the center.

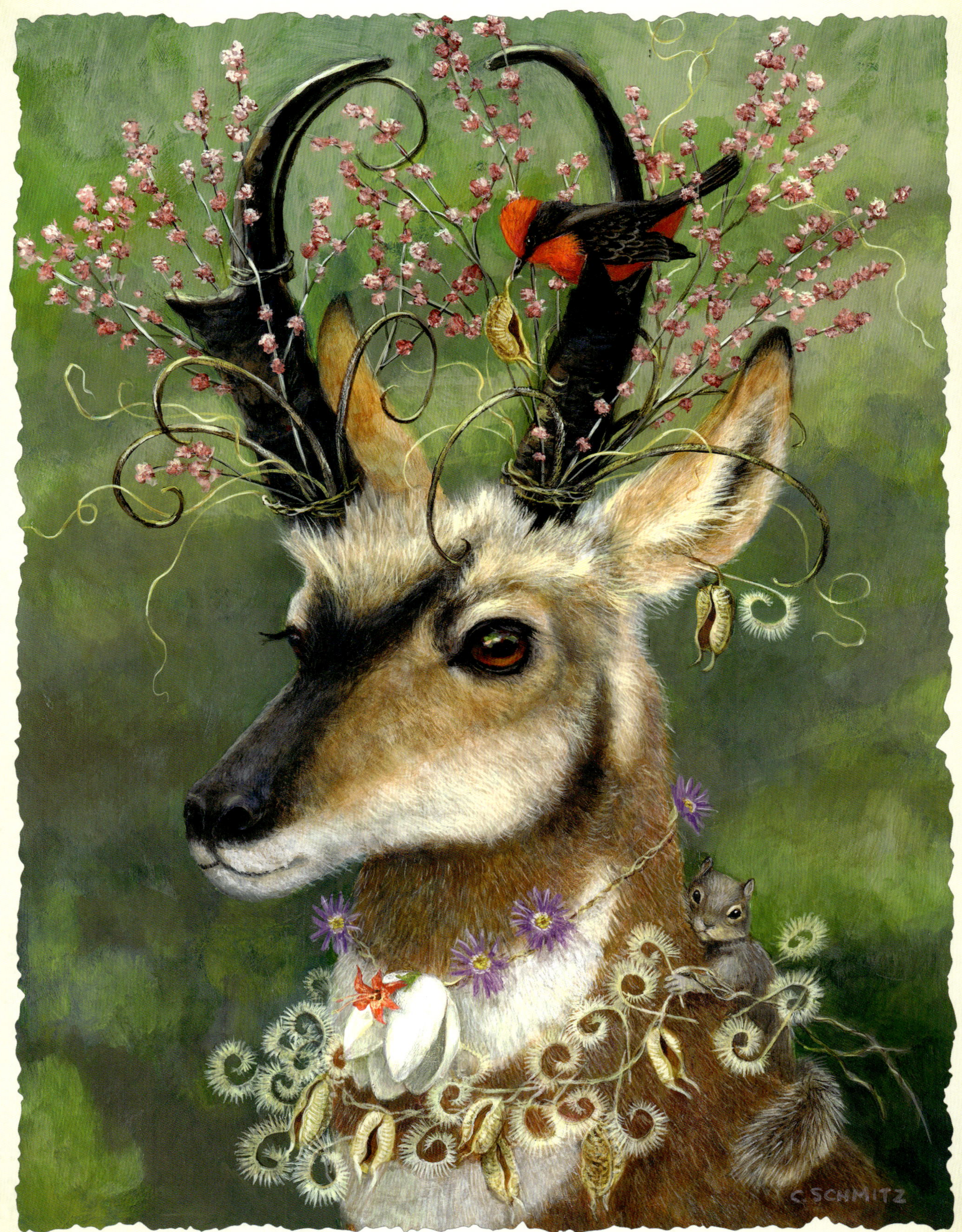
C. SCHMITZ

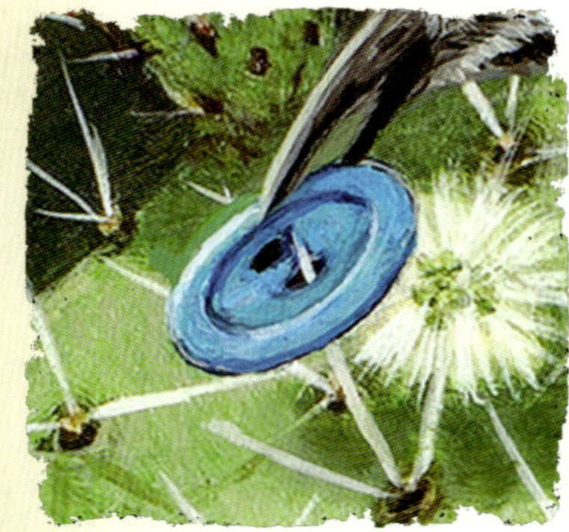

A javelina girl, feeling as lackluster as the husk of an old cholla, sat spellbound by the beauty of a large prickly pear cactus smothered with hundreds of luxuriant blooms.

"If only I could be so lovely!" she exclaimed.

A Cactus Wren, busily tinkering with a mass of twigs, paused and cocked his head at her.

"I am a master craftsman," he said. "Let's make you shine!"

Choosing a plump cactus pad for a broad-brimmed hat, he worked magic with bits of acacia, desert fern, fairy duster, creosote, devil's claws, snakeskins, and even scorpion tails. He pierced her ear with barrel cactus spines, then topped it all with a curious blue gem.

"It must be the snout of a toy piglet—perfect for one as pretty as you."

The javelina girl beamed.

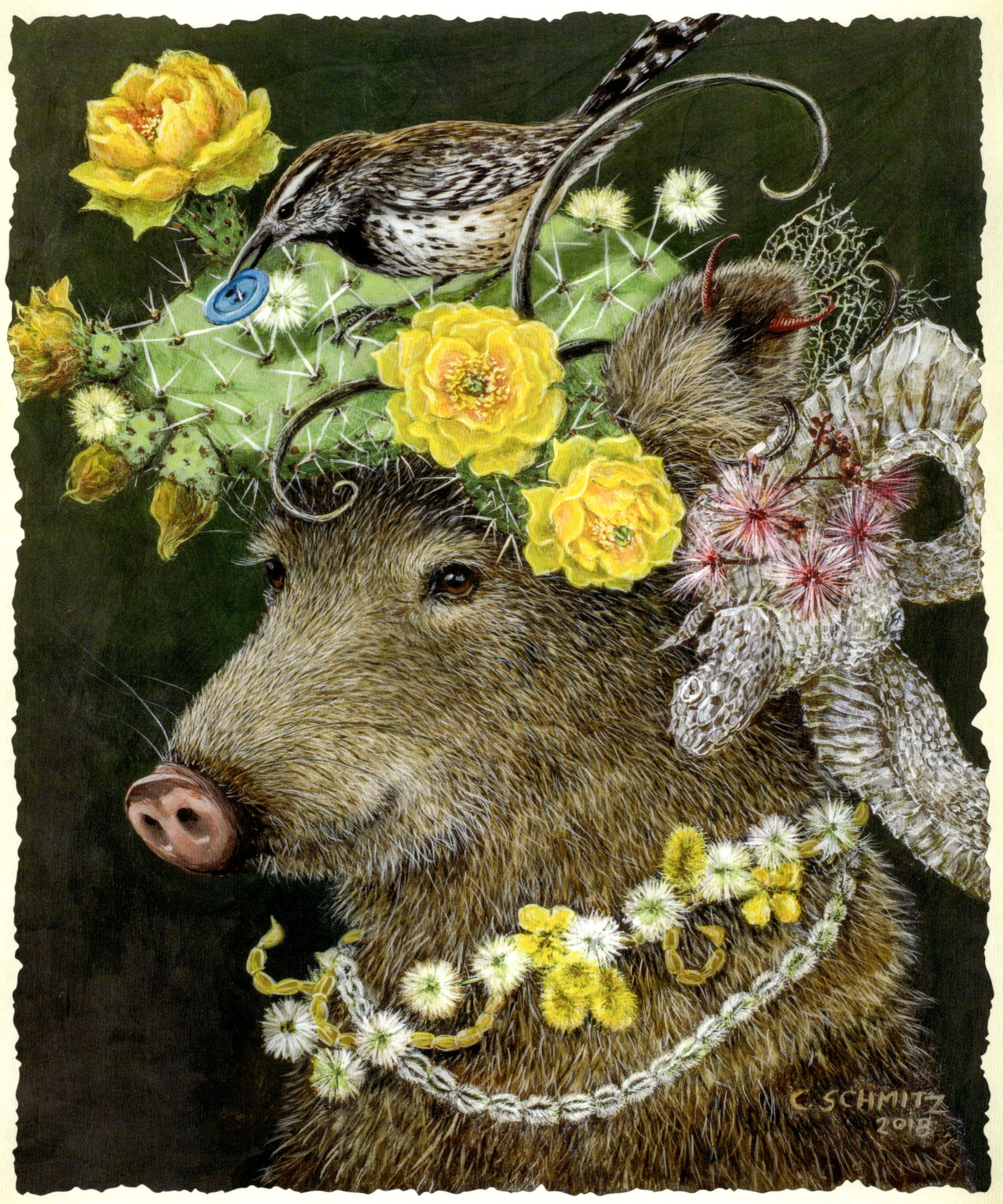
C. SCHMITZ
2018

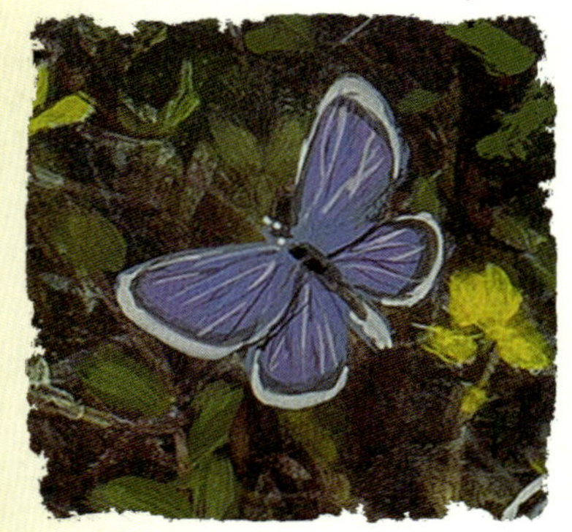

Screened by bursage and creosote, a gray fox observed the erratic motion of the crowd, unsure whether it would be wise to come out. An untamed mix of Apache plumes, desert fern blossoms, devil's claws, and lacy cactus fiber rested lightly between his ears.

"With my following of free-spirited Antillean blues, I would be spotted soon enough," he sighed.

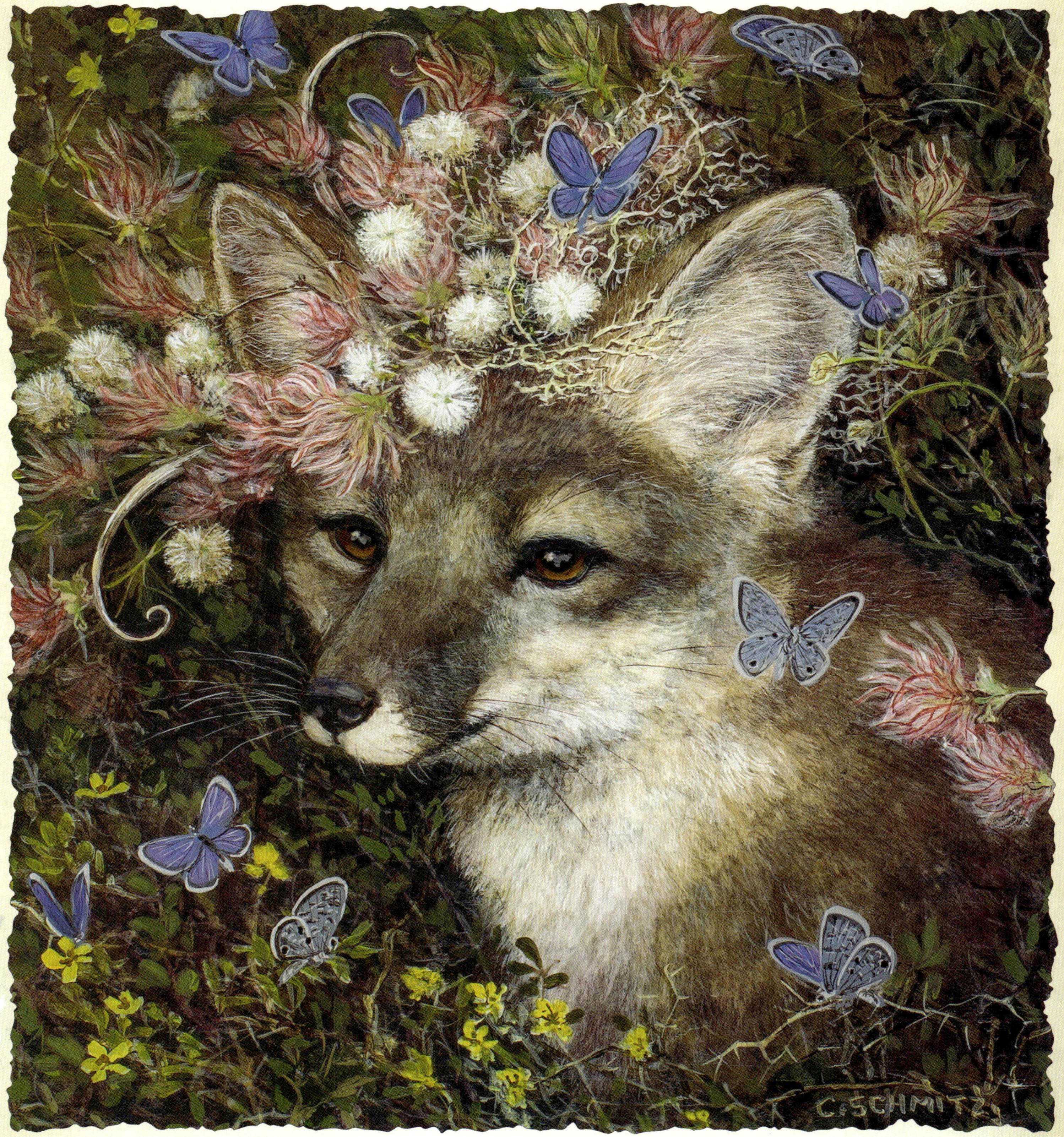

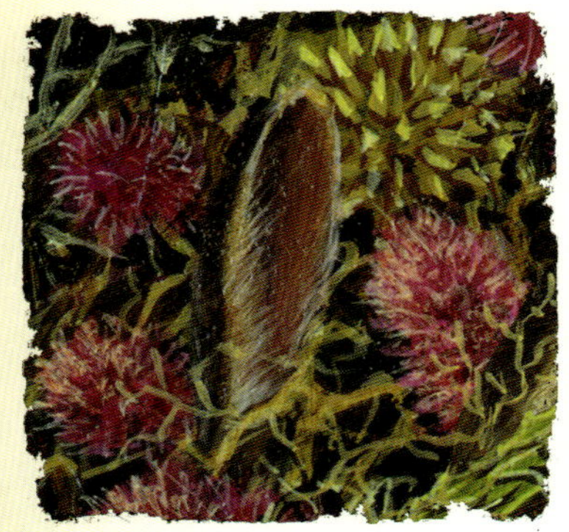

In late afternoon, from down Mexico way, a jaguar emerged from the chaparral. Already a ravishing beauty in her spots alone, she wore a wild sombrero—an organ pipe cereus flower, afloat in a mass of cactus fiber, with velvetpod mimosa and gently waving sotol leaves. Datura pods and catclaw acacia strung on yucca fiber encircled her neck. She, too, had the audacity to scooch in the ears of a desert cottontail.

The rabbits dashed for cover.

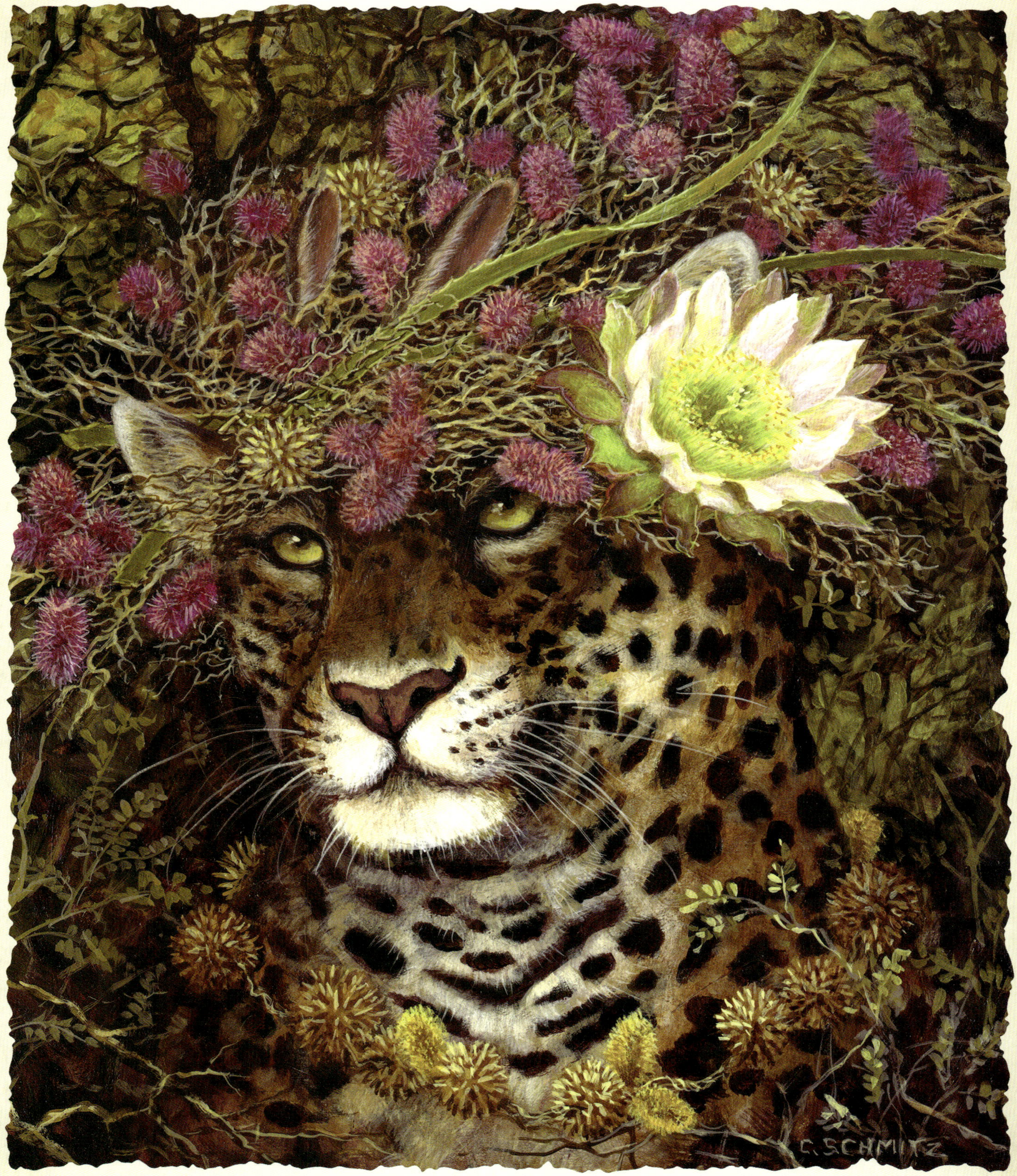

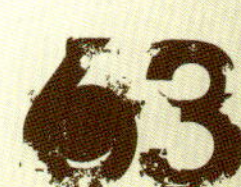

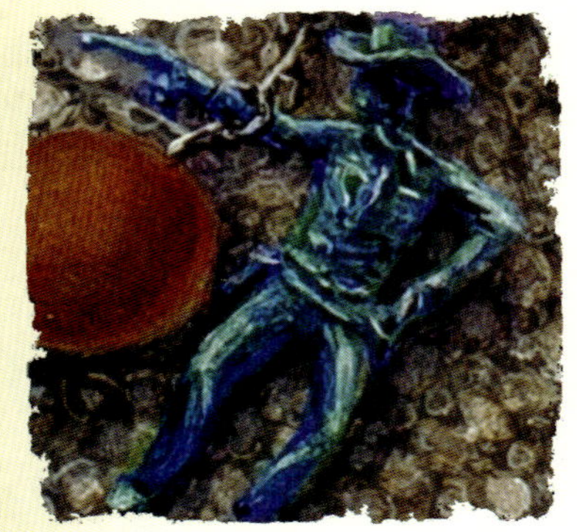

A footloose armadillo and a pocket mouse had set out on a scavenger hunt and lost their way. Meandering westward along roadsides and watercourses, they collected wildflowers and curiosities—Texas ebony, bluebonnets, acacia, blanket flowers, bluebells, oak galls, cactus fruits, and snakeskins. The mouse made a pinkie ring from a scorpion's tail and poked a tiny bone through one ear. Even a plastic cowboy was slipped in.

Most peculiar was the shiny red object from another armored creature—a 1958 Chevy Impala!

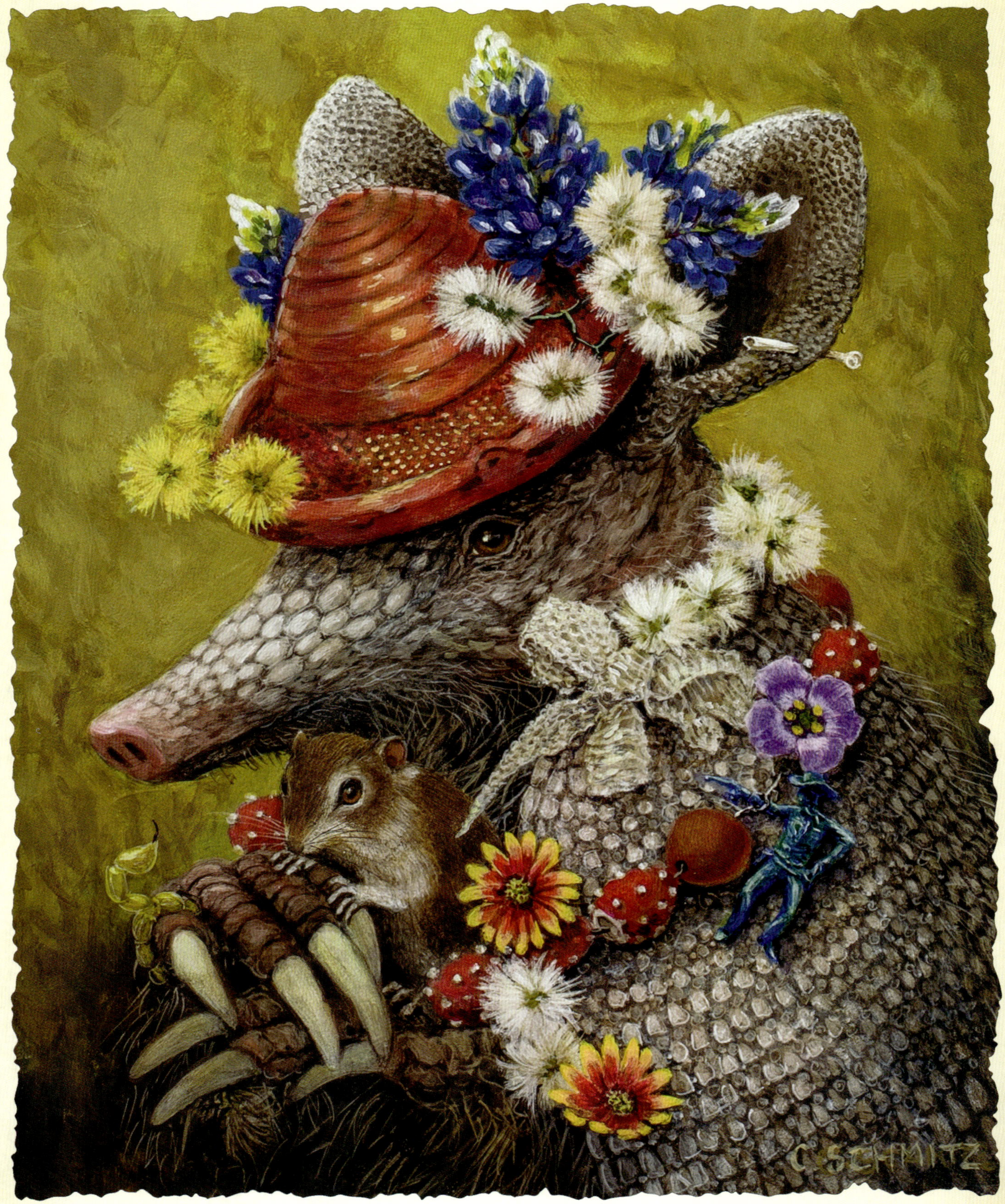

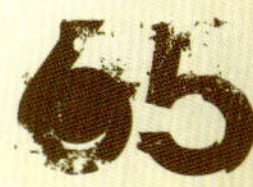

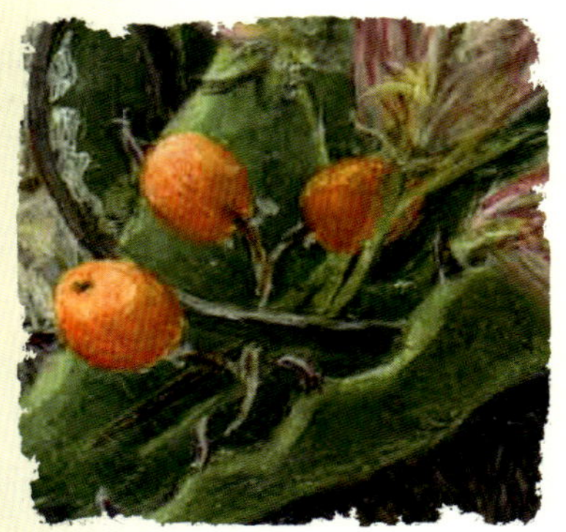

"Look at that floozy," murmured a gray fox as a gaudily dressed raccoon made her entrance. Billowing between her ears were agave leaves, devil's claws, cane beardgrass, hackberries, Apache plumes, and ribbons of snakeskins. She waved a coordinating fan and scarf. Bejeweled with the legs and elytra of June beetles, she had first savored their creamy insides.

"She definitely over-accessorized," agreed another fox.

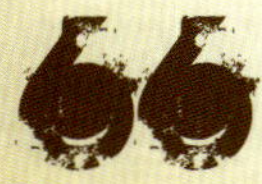

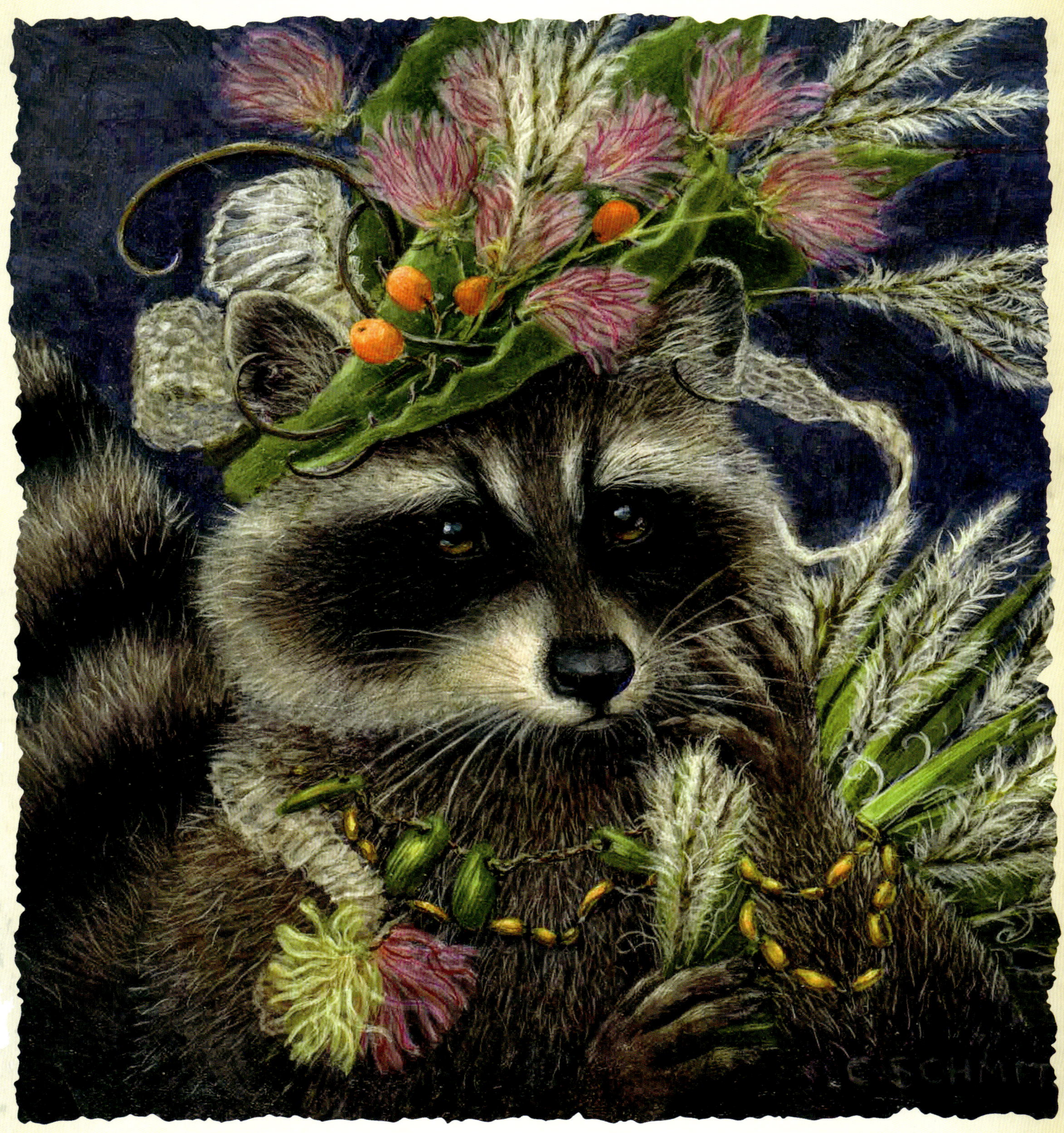
C SCHMIT

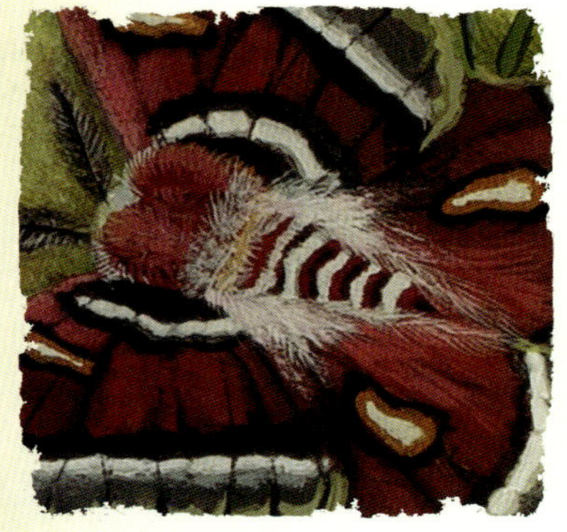

A bobcat's eyes shone with the verdant hues of her cap and ruff. Fuzzy mullein leaves with forest trimmings—pine needles, pussy willows, acorns, and yarrow—blended with her soft fur. A mere spot on her leafy collar was a red velvet mite—a puckered vermilion pouf fringed with its legs and feelers. Cotton grass and a western dayflower guided a spectacular cecropia moth as she circled for a landing.

"Who could top this?" the bobcat boasted as the moth touched down.

The rabbits, while relieved that she had not "parted out" one of their kind for her hat, nevertheless remained vigilant.

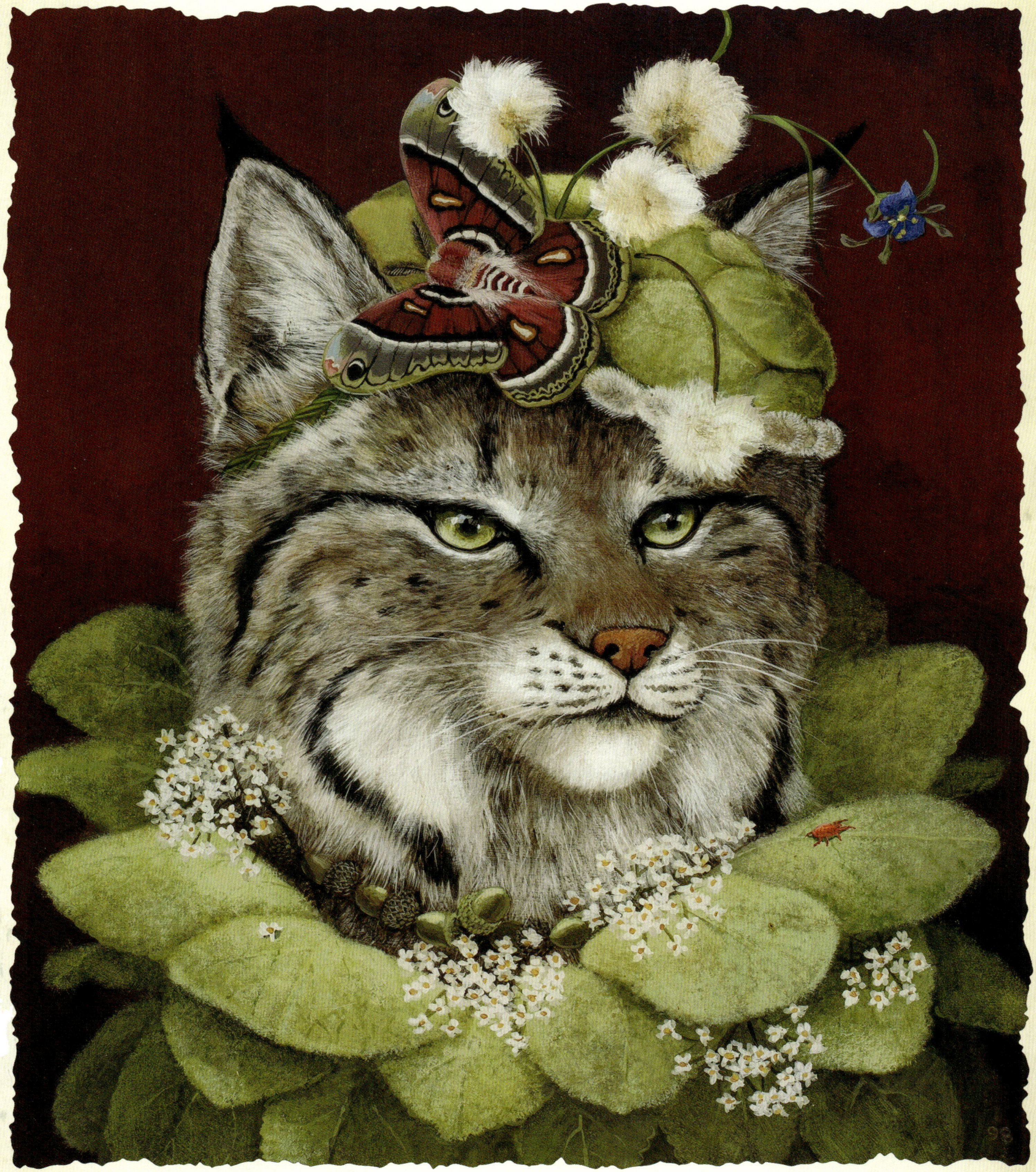

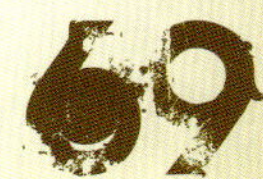

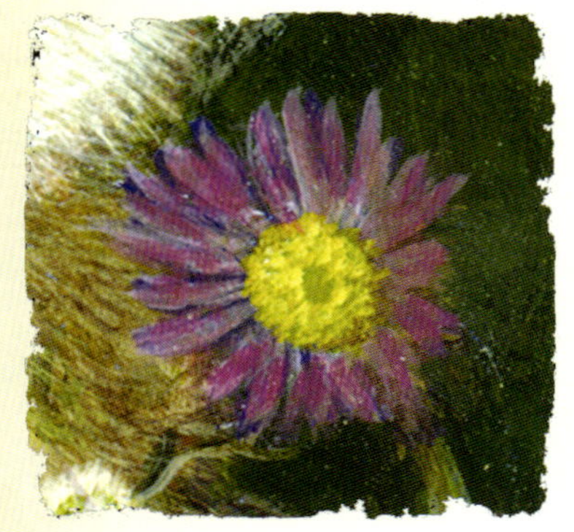

Well known for being shy and pale, a kit fox surprised everyone with an exuberant burst of color, the ultimate bling: a bloom from the southwest coral bean tree. Apache plumes, acacia blossoms, desert zinnias, creosote seeds, and a Mojave aster added more pizazz. Cleverly composed devil's claws appeared to be spinning.

"I am certainly visible now!"

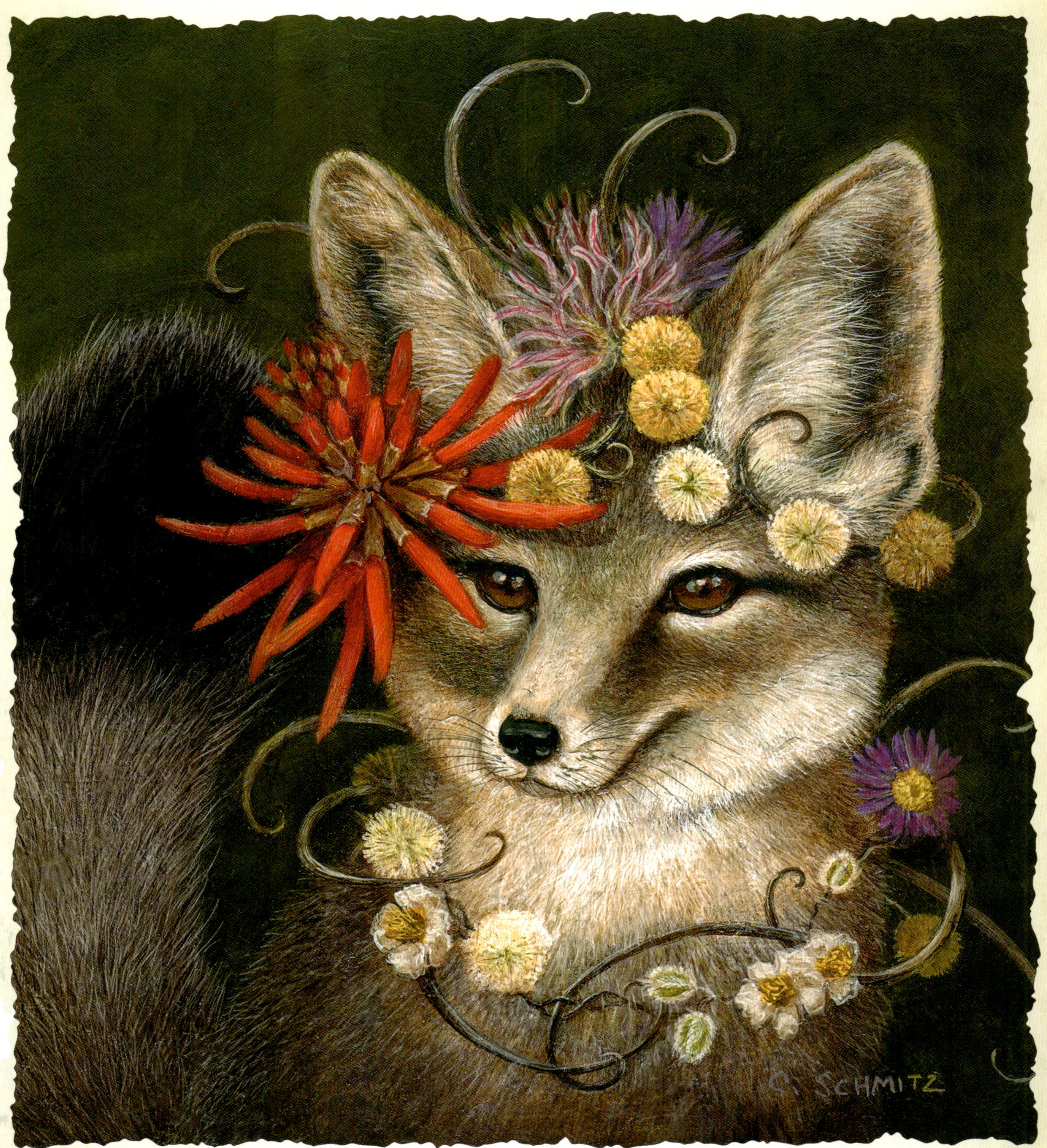
C. SCHMITZ

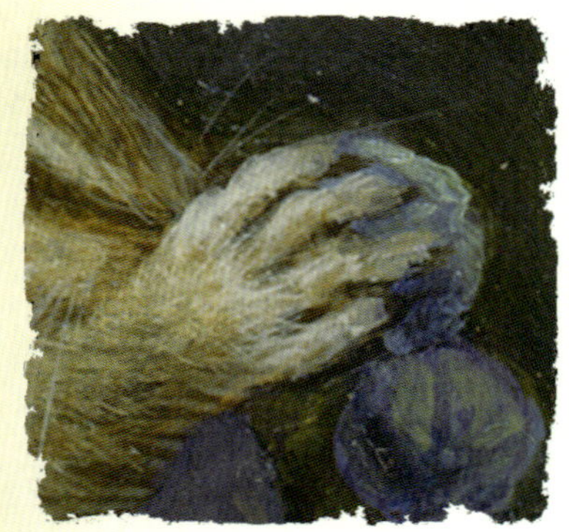

"Sunny?" Everyone was puzzled when a black-and-white nocturnal creature introduced herself.

"It's true, I do have a nightlife and sleep all day," the skunk began. "But one afternoon, on a whim, I ventured out. The autumn glow of a grape arbor made me blink. I couldn't resist plucking a big leaf. Then I noticed a jay feather in vivid blue, and multi-hued juniper berries."

Her chipmunk friend joined in. "I offered to help her gather more treasures—oak galls, dried Arizona cudweed, willow leaves, and a raven feather. Using vine tendrils, I wove them all into a necklace and a golden tiara. She looked as bright as the sun!"

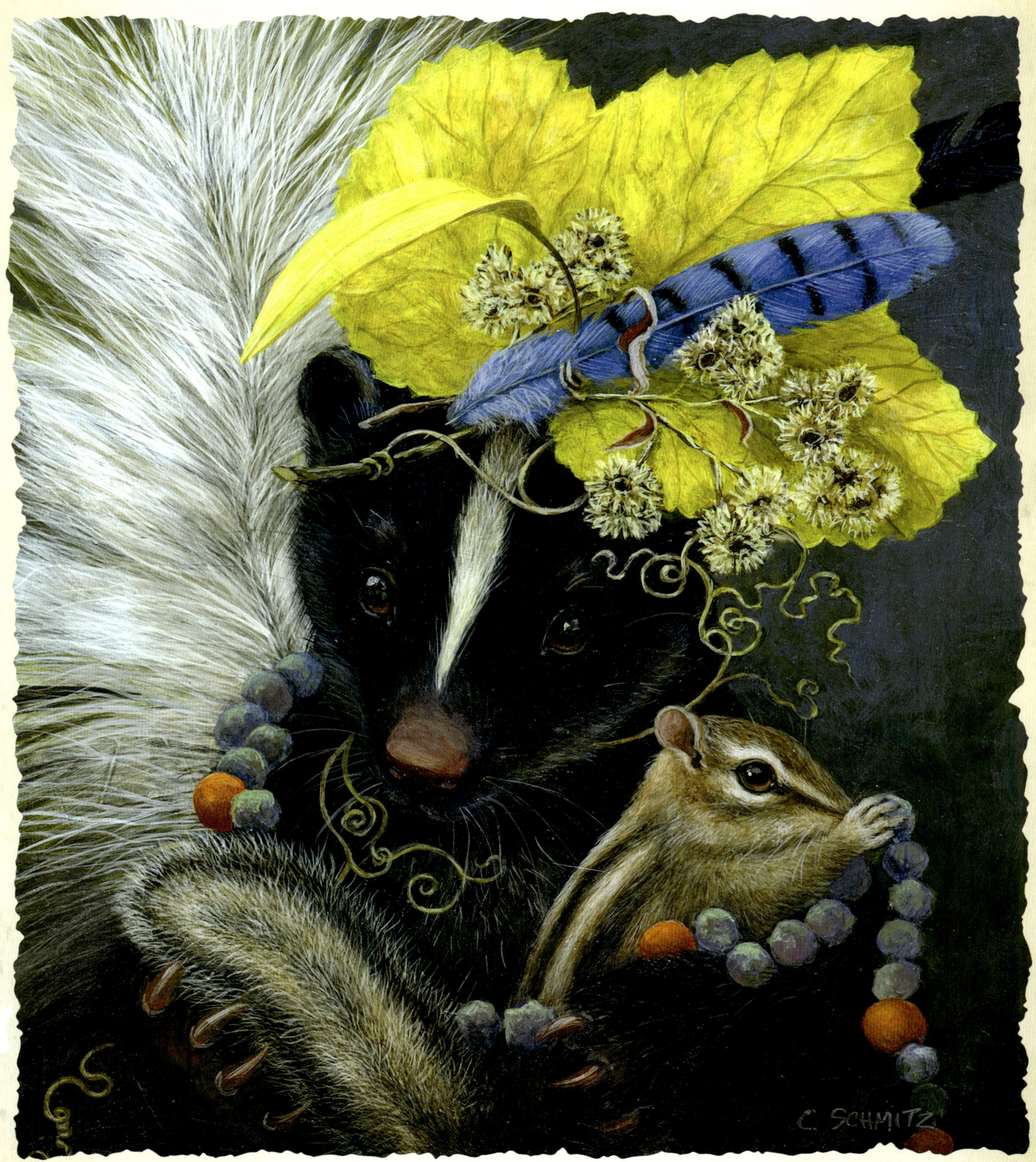
C. SCHMITZ

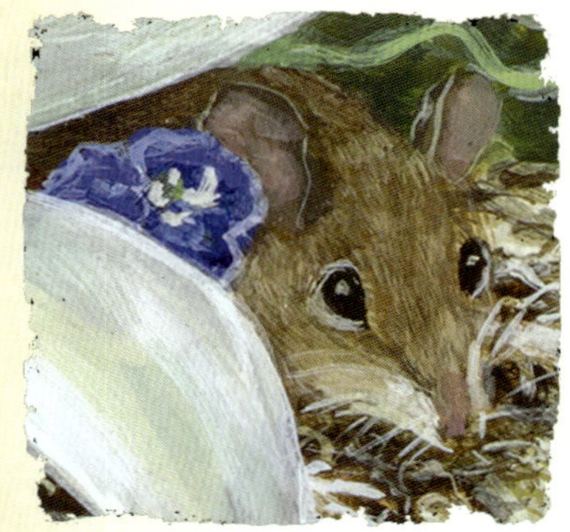

A Burrowing Owl from Ajo turned heads at the Wild Hat Celebration.

Her tree-dwelling kin were envious. Unlike them, she often puttered about among the desert shrubs in search of rodents. One evening she had come upon some low dunes illuminated by colonies of desert lilies.

"Whoooo," she whispered. "Here is THE LOOK I want!"

The owl offered safe passage to a brush mouse in exchange for his handiwork. Around the owl's shoulders he wound strands of creosote seeds, desert chicory, and feather-soft blooms of acacia and desert fern. To a pad of cactus fiber, he affixed midnight-blue desert bells, a constellation of gravel ghost flowers on their invisible stems, and finally one moon-bright lily with its long, rippling leaves.

The owl blinked her approval and the mouse crouched under a petal.

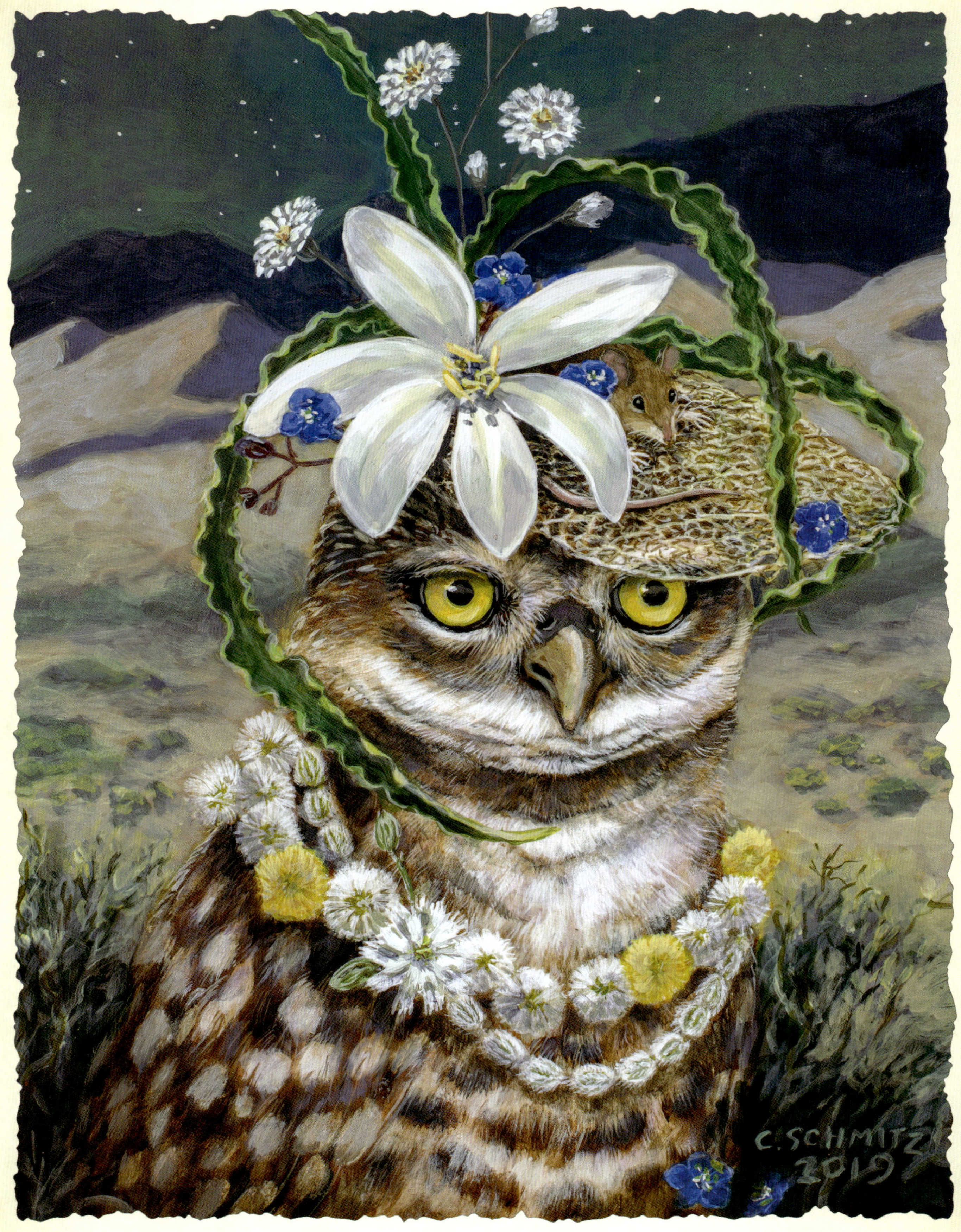
C. SCHMITZ
2019

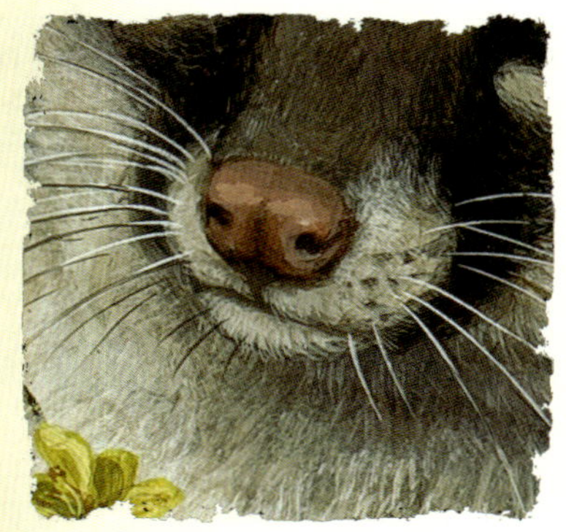

A ringtail cat displayed the striped yardage and night-vision eyes that gave her a name. A tissue-thin ruff of cactus fiber, grama grass, and chuparosa was tied with creosote flowers while its seeds adorned her wrist. Fairy duster blooms nestled in her ears enhanced her aura of sweetness.

"I'm not really a cat, or a coon," she said, "but I do share traits with each. Sometimes I am called 'Tlacomixtle.' Well, what's in a name?"

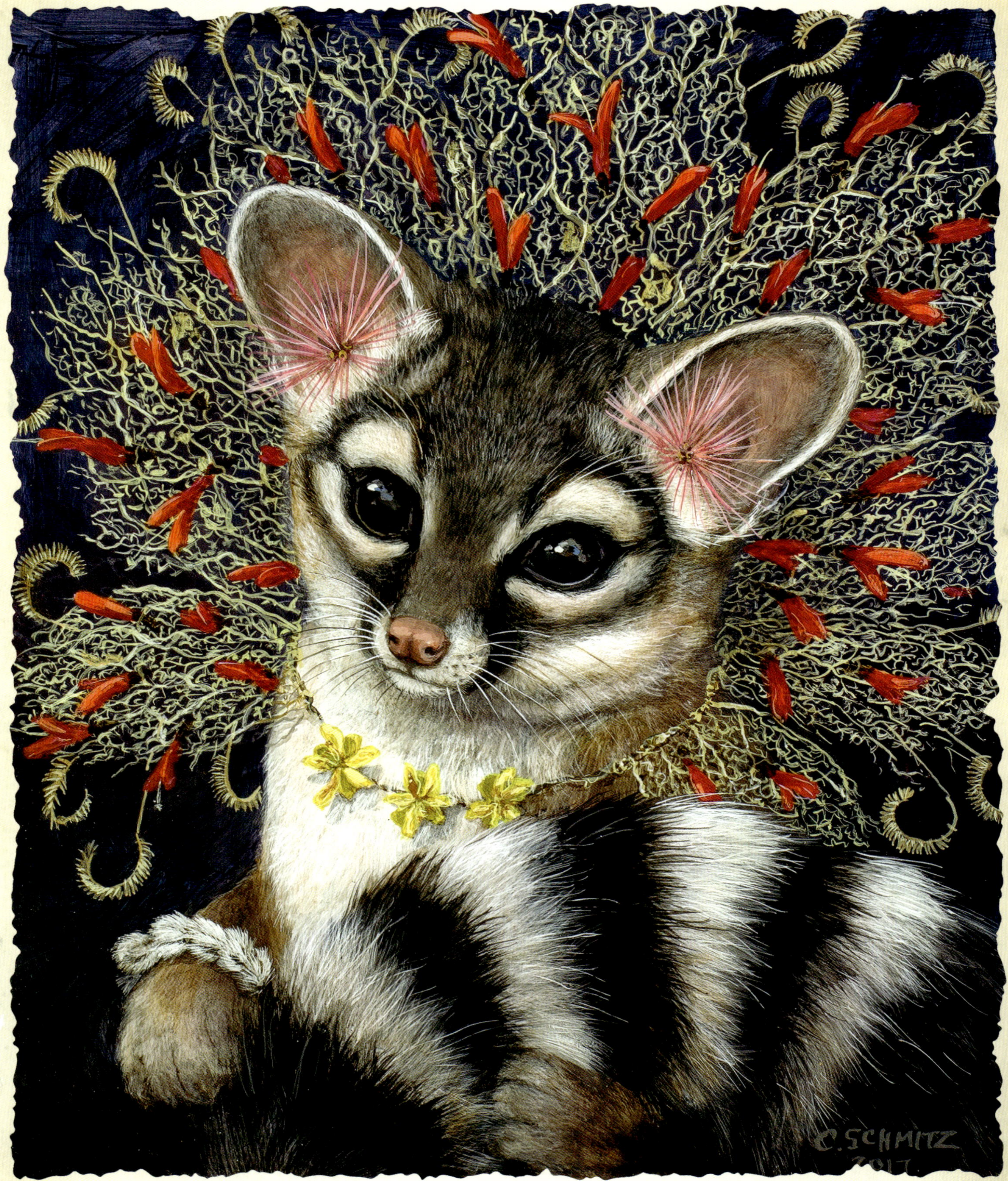

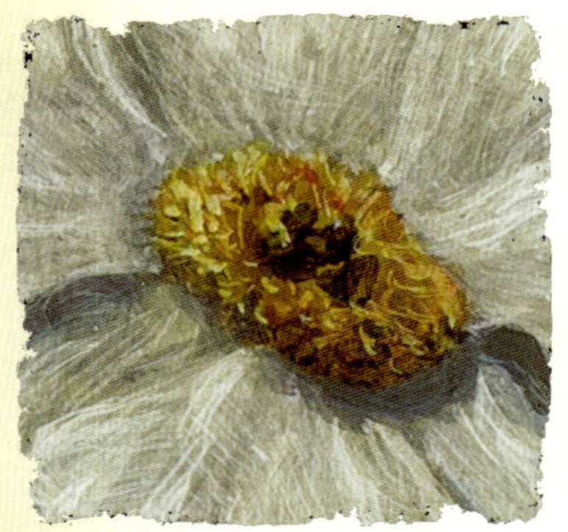

"Dude! May I take your coat and hat?" a heckler shouted as a tough-looking fellow bullied his way through the crowd. Everyone hastily moved aside, gawking at the badger.

"It's a helmet!" he growled.

The ringtail cat beside him quickly intervened. "An old headlight bucket was all he could dig up," she explained. "But I insisted on the prickly poppy. Doesn't he look fetching?"

She whisked her tail across his face, just missing the red velvet mite. The badger blushed and looked down at his fingernails.

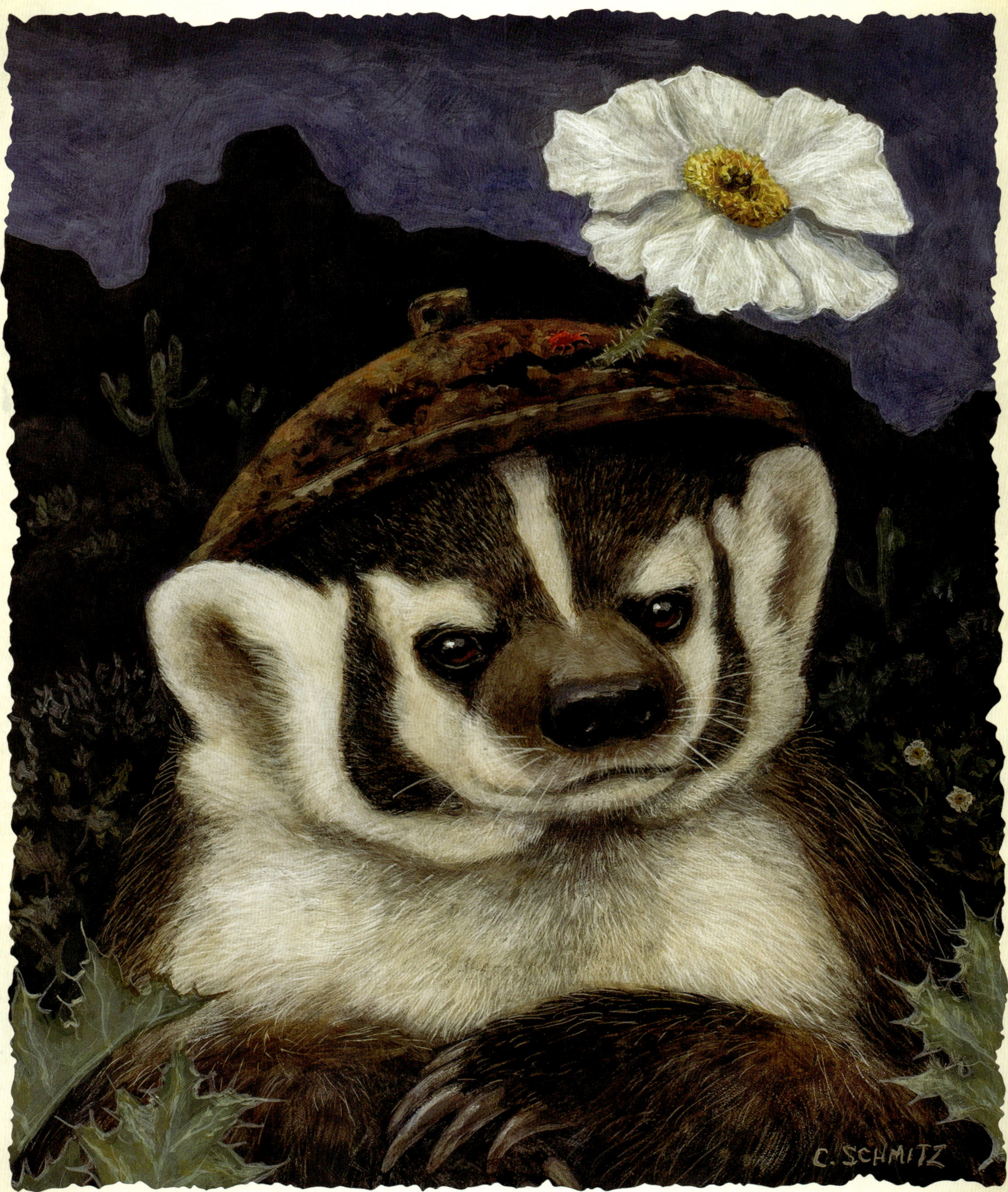
C. SCHMITZ

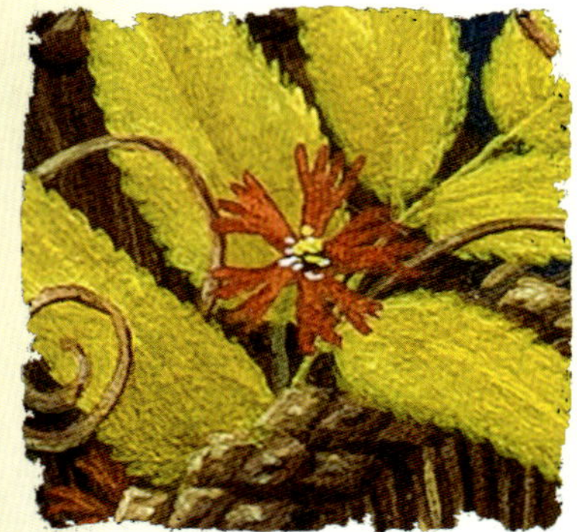

Barbeara's heart was set on a bewitching little hat to express her dark side. She was crestfallen when her request was met with blank stares from the hat makers.

"How about Art Deco?" one of them hurriedly suggested.

A Wilson's Warbler and a Northern Flicker selected oak and walnut leaves, and orange silene flowers. A chipmunk gathered grape vine tendrils, acorns, pine cone petals and rare curly pine needles. The result was a meticulously crafted cupola of geometric forms. Barbeara was tickled pink.

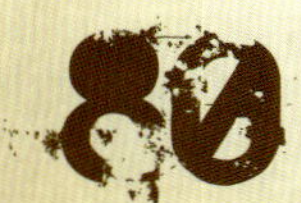

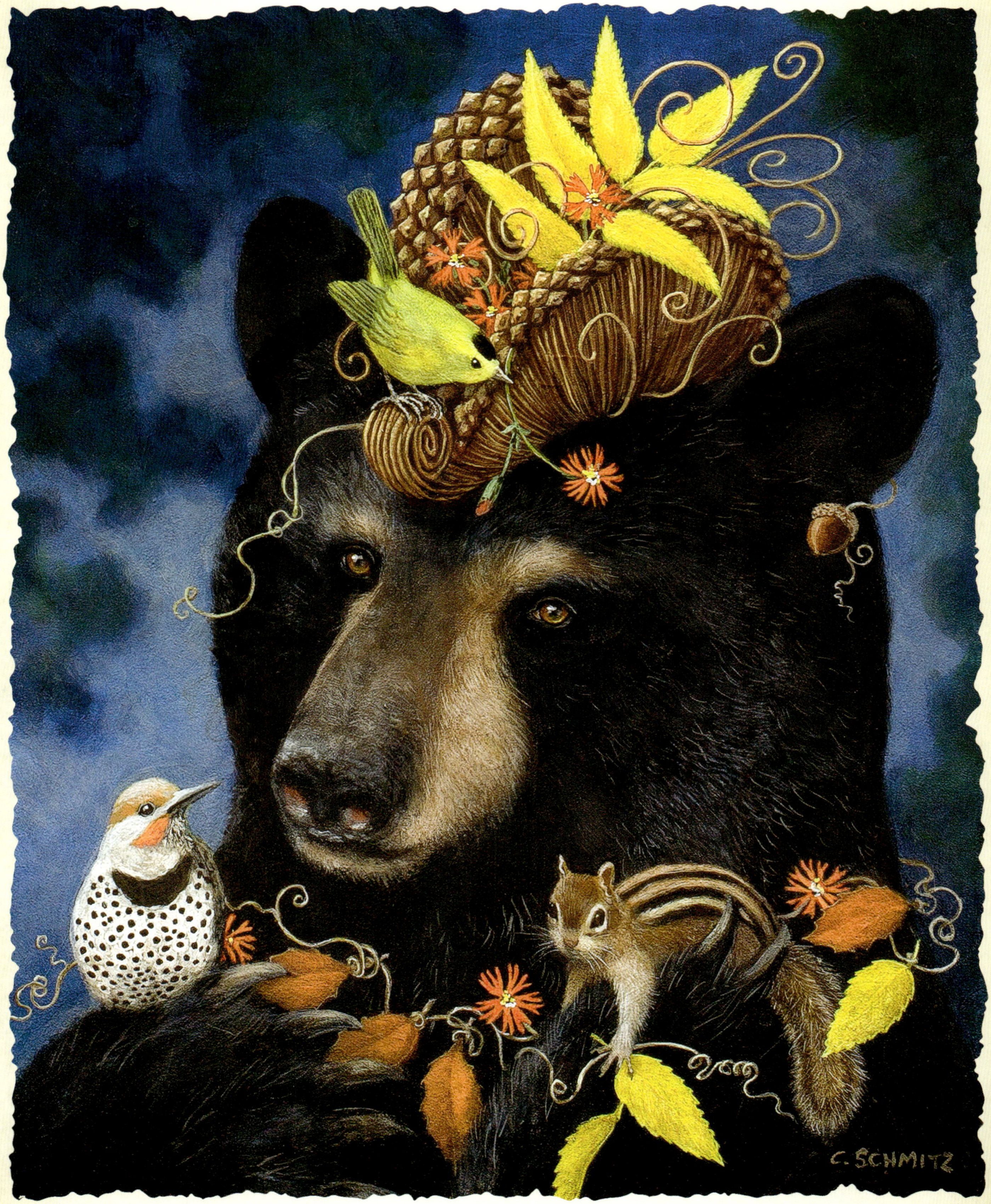

C. SCHMITZ

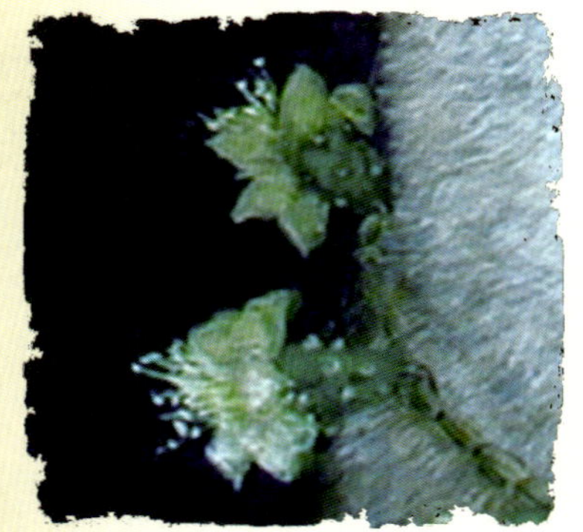

At dusk, another vain feline padded silently into the gathering. The cougar was breathtaking in the large, fragrant flower of a night-blooming cereus with golden coils of scorpion tails and twinkling cholla blossoms. Sphinx moths approached the ghostly-white flower to gather its pollen. She believed that her ensemble would outshine the others, capturing the award without her resorting to her usual tactics.

Now concerned for the quivering rabbits, the bears quietly scooted their bodies between them and the big cats. The skunks, with full tanks, went on high alert.

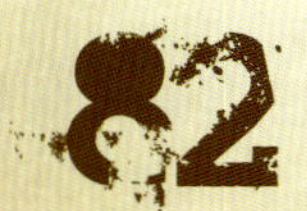

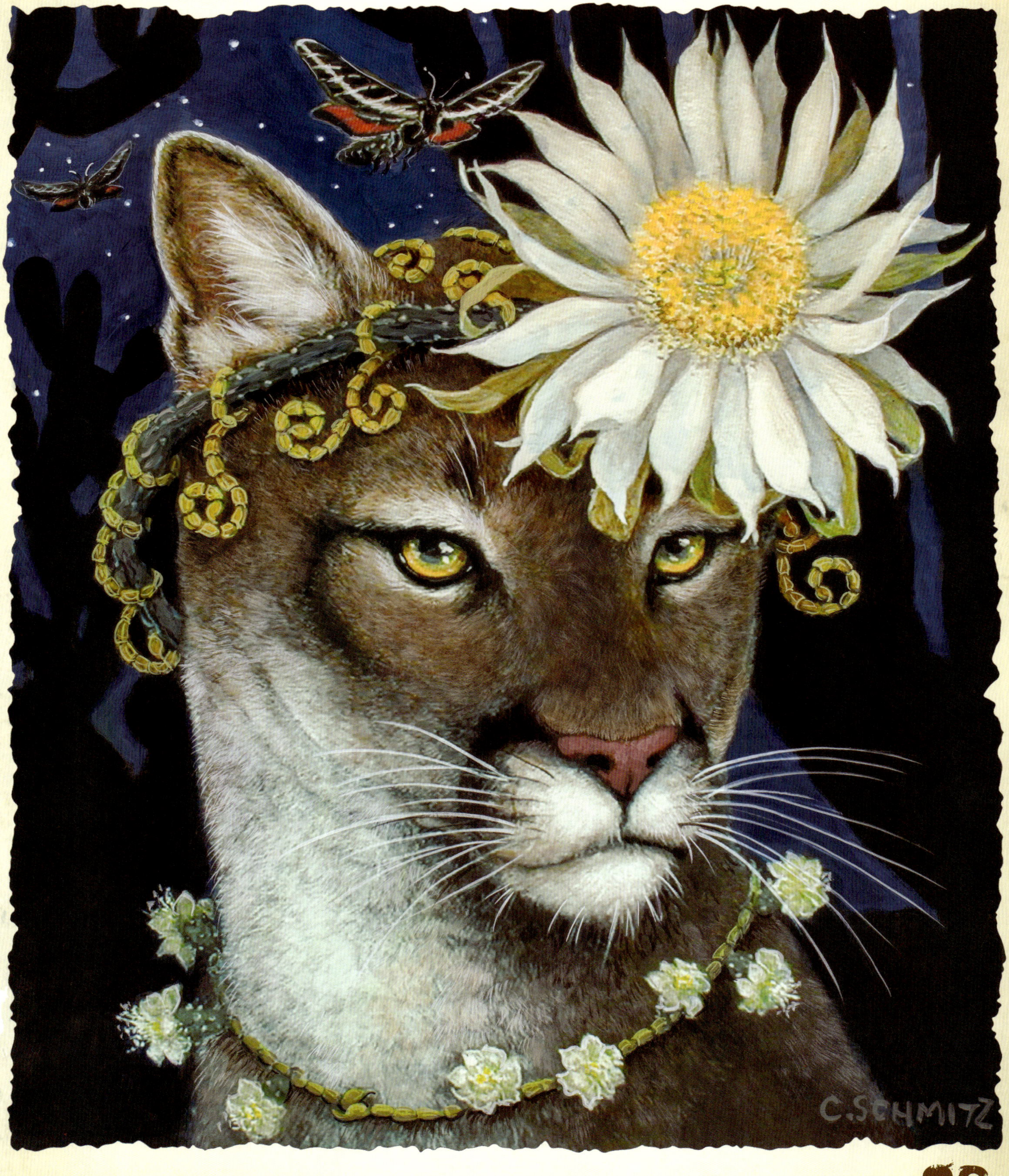

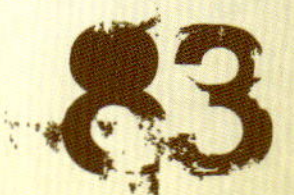

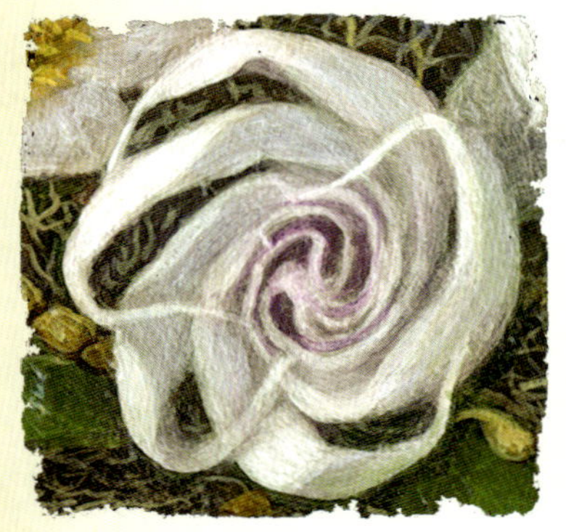

A mule deer, resplendent under the rising moon, was greeted by gasps of awe. Held in place by a lacy fretwork of cactus fiber were glowing, scented blooms of sacred datura and evening primrose with curls of scorpion tails. Dangling mesquite pods and snake rattles rustled as she moved. Aware that she could arouse the jealousy of the cats, she entwined her throat with dangerously sharp devil's claws and datura seed pods.

"To make those whiskered demons think twice," she assured herself.

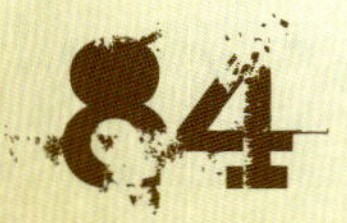

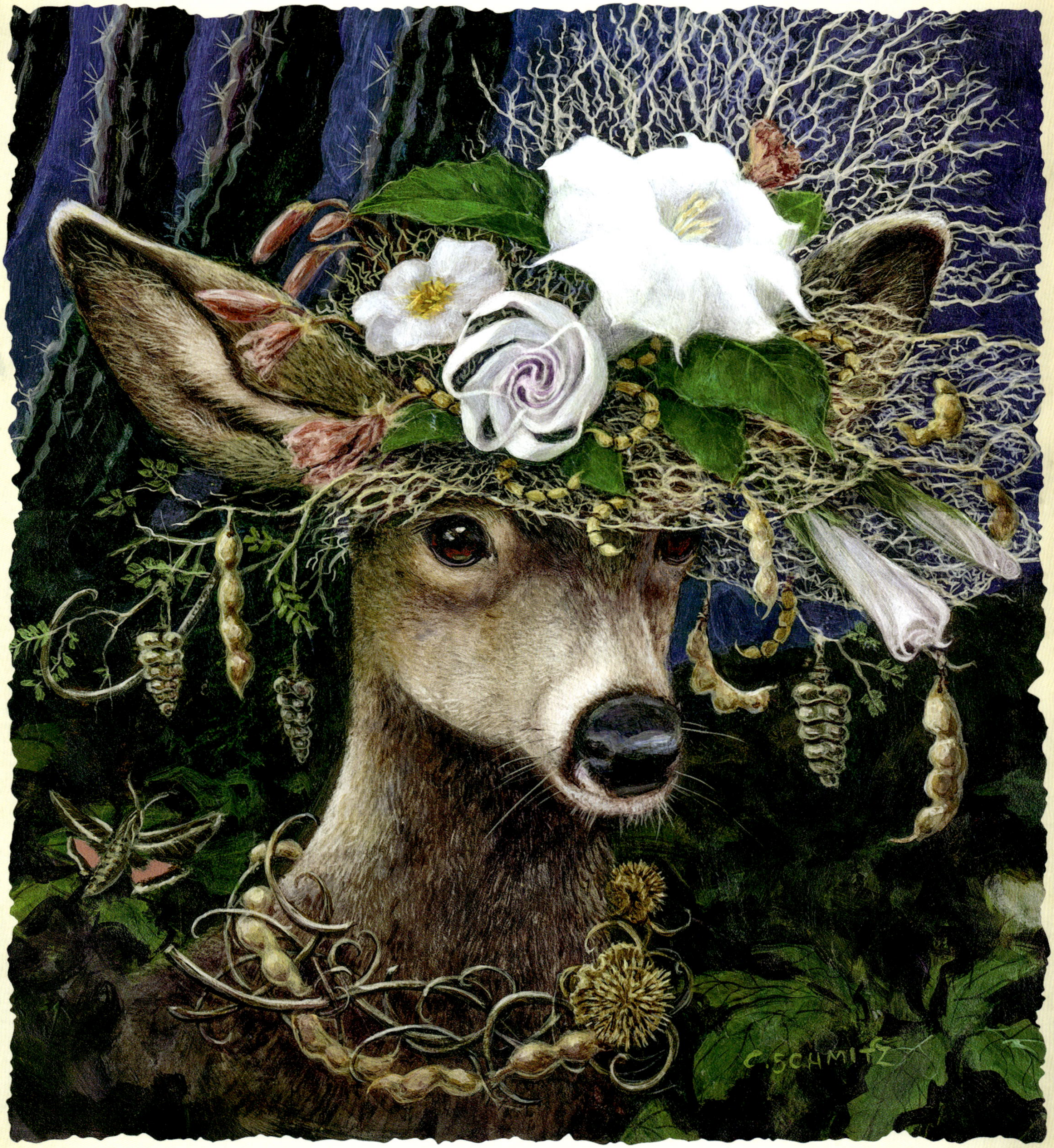

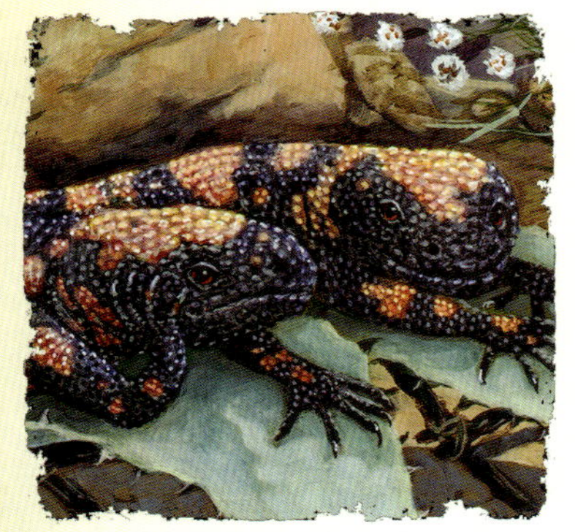

The Gila monster couple, dazzled by the display of hatted creatures, agreed that choosing a winner from this bumptious crowd would be as easy as clambering up a giant saguaro to feast on birds' eggs. They also knew, in their ancient wisdom, that mayhem could ensue.

"Who started all this?" she asked.

"Those upstart ravens," he griped. "Another feather-brained caprice that we 'monsters' must tidy up with our reliable reptilian brains. But I'm getting some good vibes. Let's see how it goes."

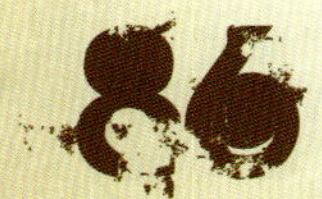

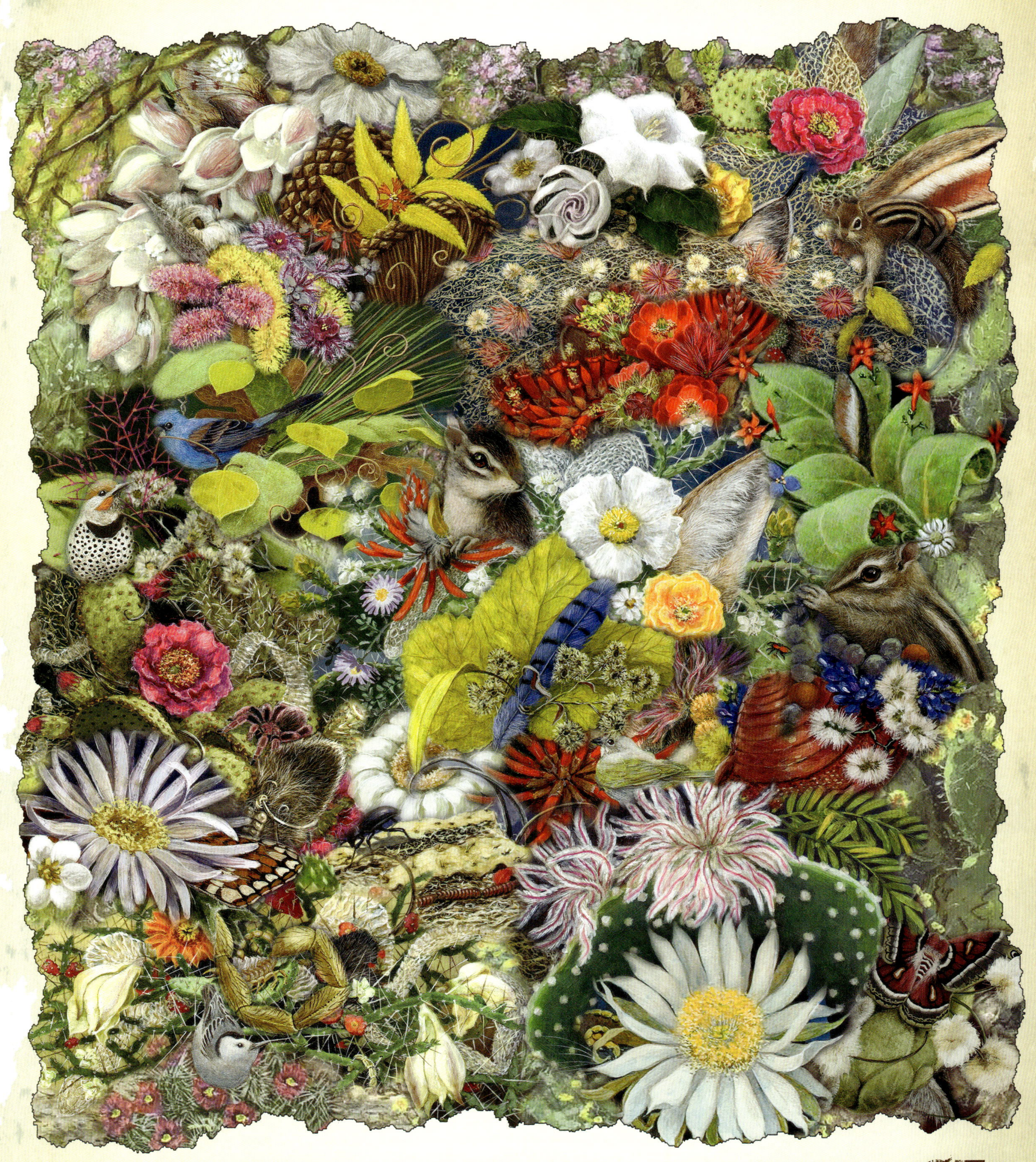

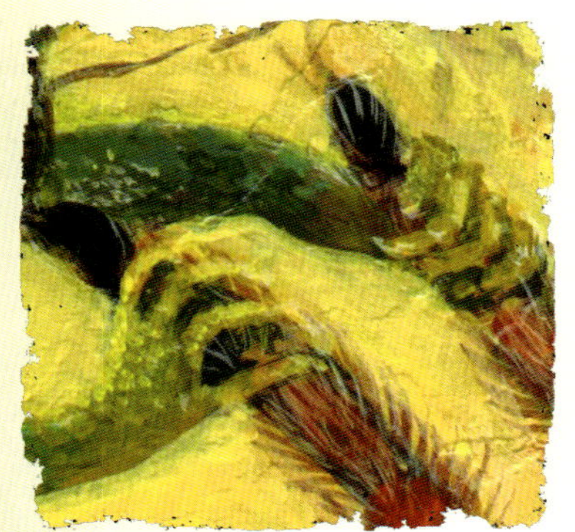

Surprisingly, the revelers were indeed becoming more companionable than competitive. Nobody ruffled any feathers or rubbed any fur the wrong way. Nobody noticed if one hat was more quirky or gorgeous than another. They were seeing each flower, leaf, twig, thorn, berry, or bug with new eyes.

Animals who normally avoided each other—or ate each other—found much to share. They told stories, "talked shop", or expressed their secret dreams. Many spun around in funky dances, while others simply sat together looking at the moon, their personal cares forgotten.

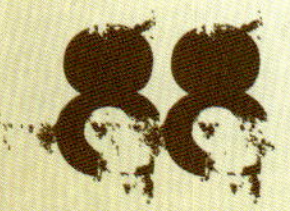

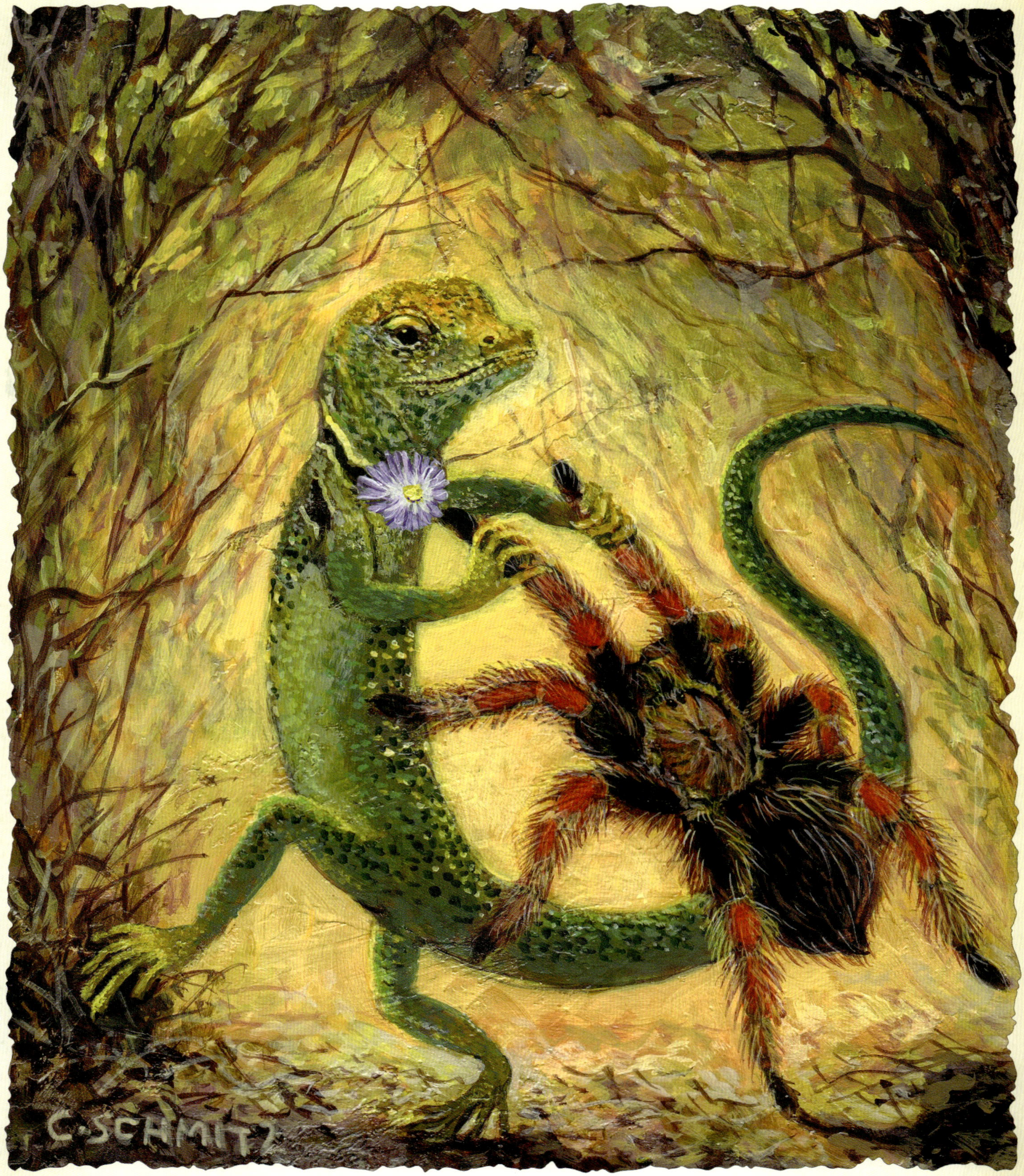

C·SCHMITZ

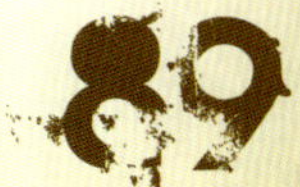

By late afternoon the following day, euphoria had been displaced by hunger pangs. Many hats, as well as their owners, had begun to look quite toothsome. It was time for herbivores and carnivores alike to straggle home and resume their usual practices of survival. Competition for food, not fashion, was the order of the day.

The spiny warrior and the Gila gent searched everywhere for the belly dancer, but she had vanished like a puff of gold dust. Perhaps they had been hallucinating.

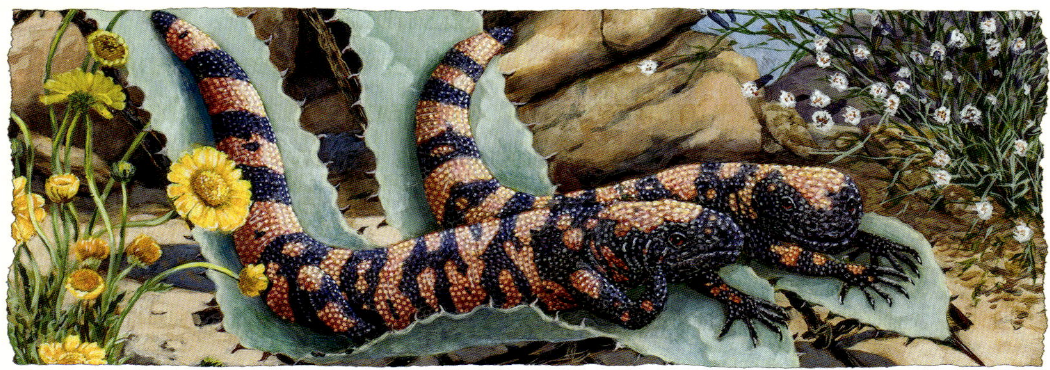

An early evening chill roused the Gila monster elders from their reverie. After a snack of spicy red ants, they wiggled into their burrow. Feeling content as they changed into matching twilight-and-blush archipelago print pajamas, they flumped into bed. They closed their eyes to dream until the sun rose on another typical day.

Yet even now there lingered a new sense in the air. Predator and prey, feeling at one with each other, had remembered that their common "ground" was the nourishment and beauty that grew out of it, their vast botanical garden once called Eden.

THE END

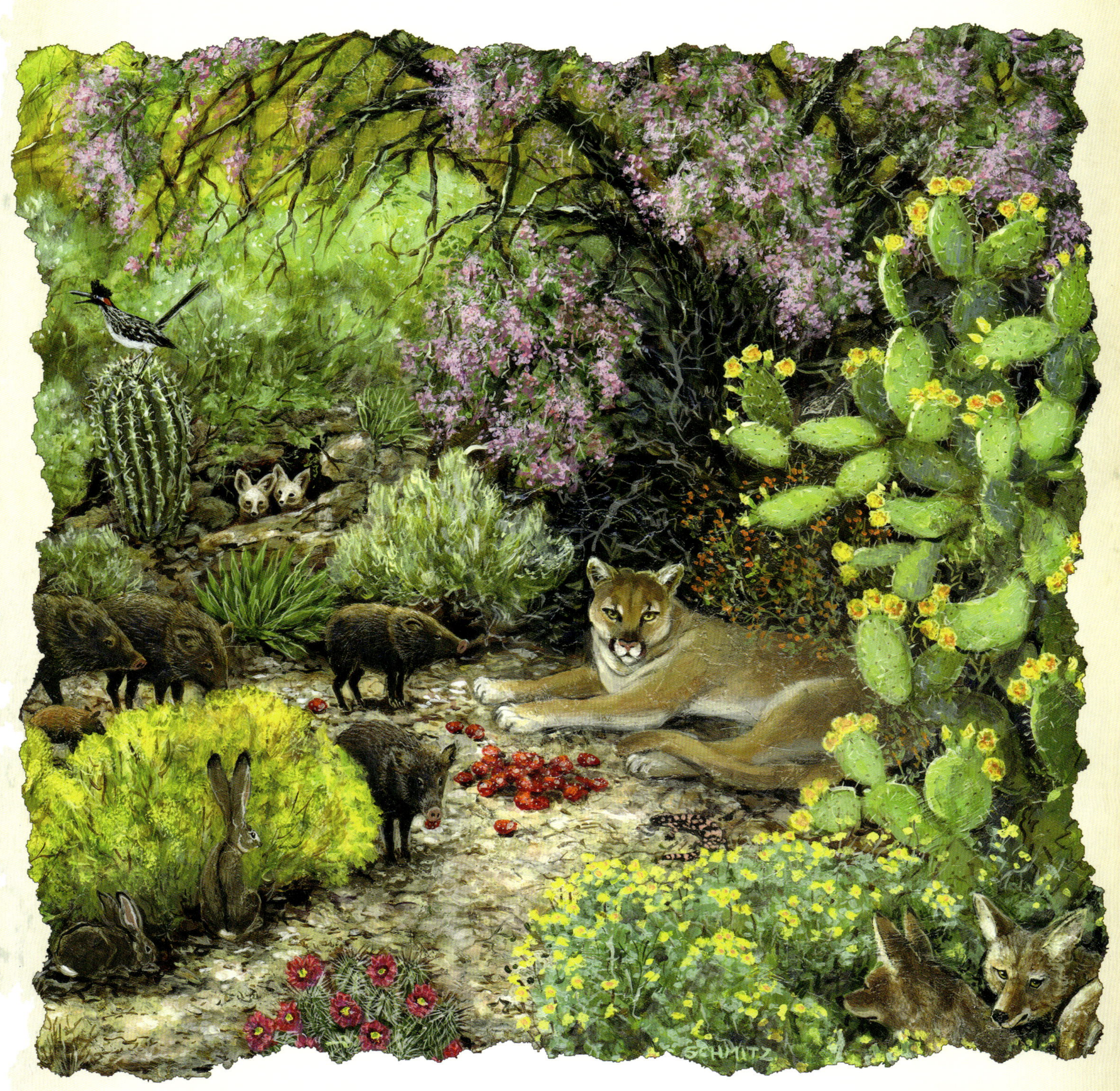
SCHMITZ

EPILOGUE

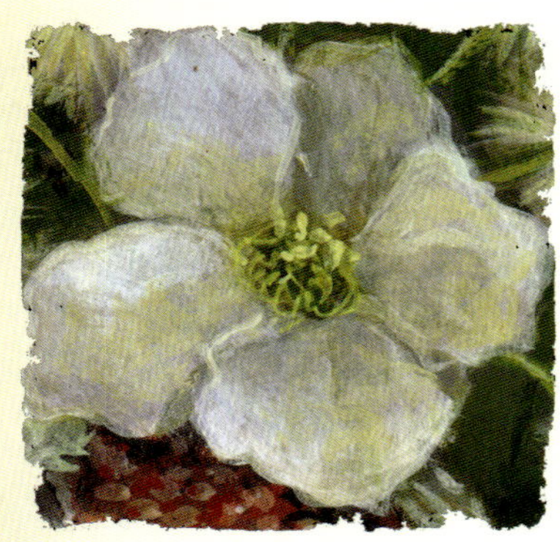

Several weeks after her performance, the belly dancer dressed up for a more intimate occasion—her wedding day! When could a Gila "monster" be any lovelier? In a veil of snakeskin organza and a halo of desert blossoms, she smiled at her beloved, a Gila Woodpecker. He had first spotted her from his saguaro penthouse. She was sunbathing on a rock below, her body shimmering with beads of coral and indigo. Enchanted, he knew instantly that she would be his forever. Now, dashing and proud in his necklace of scorpion tails, he offered her a supreme delicacy—a hummingbird's egg. Her dainty fingers twirled a garland of creosote seeds in anticipation.

Together, they will reach for the stars!

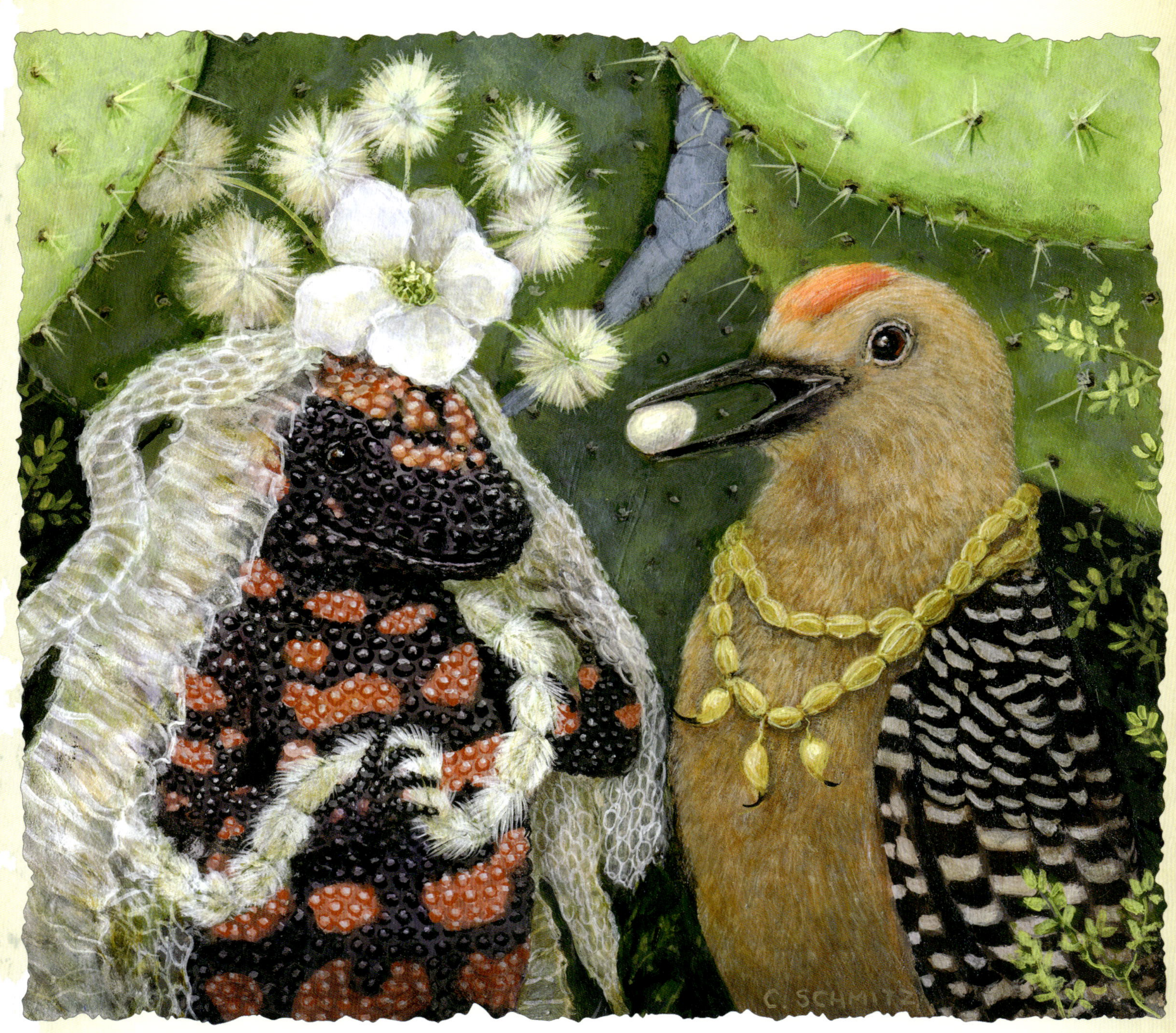
C. SCHMITZ

THE PAINTINGS

GRATITUDE

From the beginning I was blessed with an art-friendly family. My grandmother Mary Alice Smith found ways to bring art into her home on a shoestring budget. My mother Pauline did the same. My aunt Jan and uncle Bill Cantrell took me into an already full house so that I could get a start at the Kansas City Art Institute.

This book could not have come into being without the many talents, tireless labor, patience, and loving support of my brother Tony. He designed, proofed, critiqued, edited, suggested, listened and marketed. My sister Linda Schmitz-Leigh was always available for her astute insights and humor. Nothing passed without her approval. Experienced writers Stephanie Waxman, Deirdre Nunan, Liz Hufford, Karena Rice and proofreader Holly Fenelon were generous with their time in reading the manuscript and offering valuable advice. Many friends made comments and suggestions. Loyal patrons pestered me to do a book.

For turning my paintings into digital images I am indebted to Patrick Leigh and Alan Lade.

And finally, I am humbly grateful to Gary H. Wright for his extraordinary generosity.

To all of you—THANK YOU!

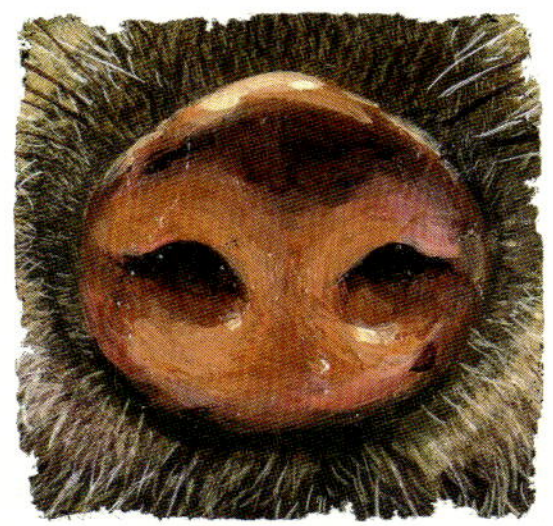

AFTERWORD

When identifying the plant material featured in this book, I used a mix of family, generic, and common names for the purpose of smoother reading. My aim was to inspire interest, fascination, and wonder. Readers may then delve into scientific detail to whatever extent they wish.

Many of these plants are officially "endangered," but rather than point them out here, I would urge us to be aware that due to habitat loss and changes in climate, many more are joining them on the path to extinction every year. As the most important life form on the earth, plants need our support and protection.

I hope this book does not become a eulogy, but rather endures as a celebration of biodiversity!

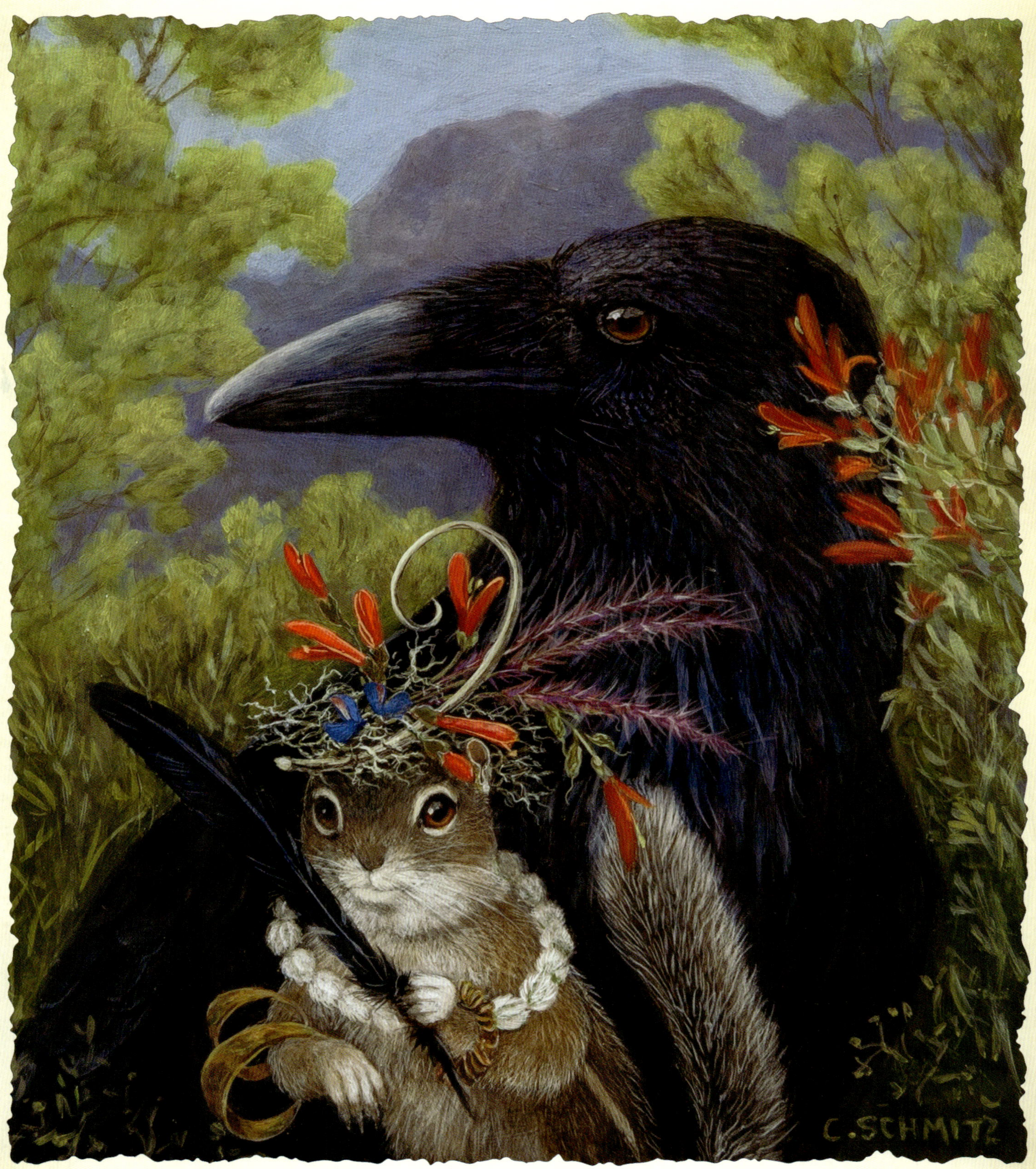
C.SCHMITZ

DESERT DADA®

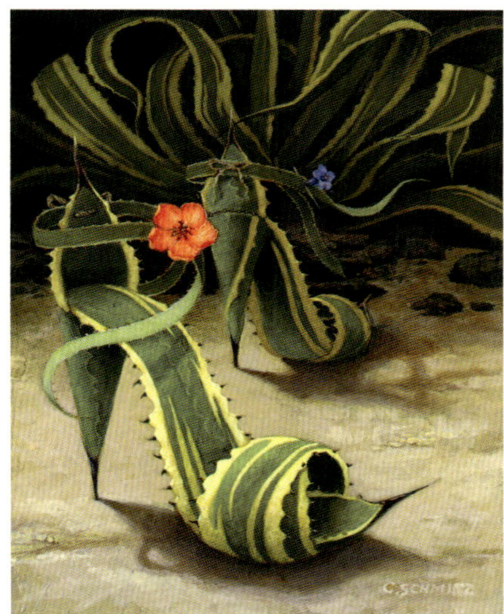

Carolyn Schmitz Fine Art

Nearly all of the images in "The Wild Hat" are available as reproductions and greeting cards.

For more about the artist, visit desertdada.com

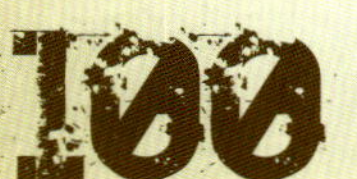